G₃

D0778684

H4
1999

HENRY DRUMMOND

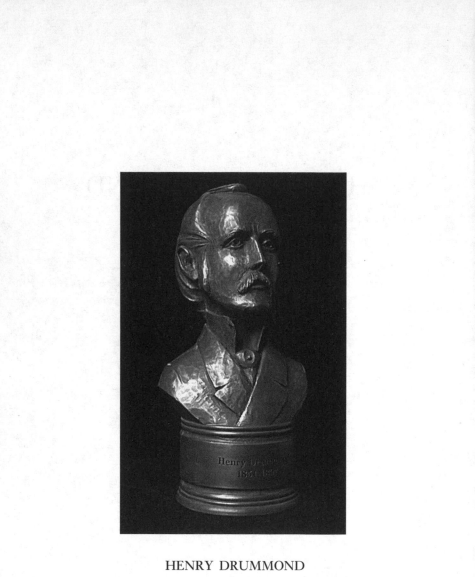

HENRY DRUMMOND
by
Glynn Acree

Sculpture copyright © 1997, Glynn Acree

HENRY DRUMMOND

A Perpetual Benediction

❧

Essays to Commemorate the Centennial of His Death

❧

Edited by
THOMAS E. CORTS

Colo. Christian Univ. Library
8787 W. Alameda Ave.
Lakewood, CO 80226

T&T CLARK
EDINBURGH

T&T CLARK LTD
59 GEORGE STREET
EDINBURGH EH2 2LQ
SCOTLAND

www.tandtclark.co.uk

Copyright © T&T Clark Ltd, 1999

All rights reserved. No part of this publication may be reproduced,
stored in a retrieval system, or transmitted, in any form or by any means,
electronic, mechanical, photocopying, recording or otherwise,
without the prior permission of T&T Clark Ltd.

First published 1999

ISBN 0 567 08667 4

British Library Cataloguing-in-Publication Data
A catalogue record for this book is available from the British Library

Caio Christian Univ. Library

Typeset by Waverley Typesetters, Galashiels
Printed and bound in Great Britain by Bookcraft Ltd, Avon

To
The Reverend and Mrs. Finlay Stewart
The Reverend Doctor and Mrs. James W. Kennedy
keepers of the Drummond flame

THE HENRY DRUMMOND CENTENARY SYMPOSIUM

March 14, 1997

Martin Hall, New College
University of Edinburgh
Edinburgh, Scotland

Sponsored by Beeson Divinity School of Samford University
Birmingham, Alabama, U.S.A.
The University of St. Andrews, Scotland
New College of the University of Edinburgh, Scotland

HENRY DRUMMOND IN AMERICA: A CENTENNIAL CELEBRATION

October 16–17, 1997

Beeson Divinity School of Samford University
Birmingham, Alabama, U.S.A.

Sponsored by Beeson Divinity School of Samford University
Birmingham, Alabama, U.S.A.
The University of St. Andrews, Scotland
New College of the University of Edinburgh, Scotland

Contributors

The Very Reverend Dr. ROBIN S. BARBOUR, K.C.V.O.
Sometime Moderator of the General Assembly of the Church of Scotland
Former Professor of New Testament Studies at New College of the
University of Edinburgh and University of Aberdeen, Scotland

Professor DAVID W. BEBBINGTON
Department of History, University of Stirling, Scotland

Dr. ALEXANDER C. CHEYNE
Professor Emeritus of Ecclesiastical History
New College of the University of Edinburgh, Scotland

Dr. THOMAS E. CORTS
President, Samford University, Birmingham, Alabama,
United States of America

Mrs. THOMAS E. (MARLA HAAS) CORTS
Samford University, Birmingham, Alabama, United States of America

Dr. TIMOTHY F. GEORGE
Dean, Beeson Divinity School of Samford University, Birmingham,
Alabama, United States of America

The Reverend C. K. O. SPENCE
Former Minister, Henry Drummond Parish Church of Scotland,
Glasgow, Scotland

Contents

THE HENRY DRUMMOND
CENTENARY SYMPOSIUM

HENRY DRUMMOND IN AMERICA: A CENTENNIAL CELEBRATION

Foreword

Like a meteor against the night, the life and work of Henry Drummond (1851–1897) left an indelible impression on the latter half of the nineteenth century. Evangelist, scientist, teacher, writer, minister, and explorer, Drummond brought grace and light to every endeavor and vocation he pursued. What has been said of his fellow Scot, Robert Murray McCheyne, is also true of Henry Drummond: few persons have so greatly influenced their own and succeeding generations in so short a life.

Drummond grew up amidst the Victorian crisis of faith, a twilight age of exuberant optimism and foreboding doom before the guns of August 1914 forever shattered the myth of inevitable progress and innate benevolence. As a liminal figure who traversed the worlds of science and religion, reason and revelation, the academy and the church, Drummond experienced firsthand many of the crosscurrents of the age in which he lived. But the deepest passion of his life was neither philosophical theology nor traditional apologetics. The great theme of Drummond's life was to know Jesus Christ and to make him known to others. He could say with St. Paul, "This one thing I do," and with Kierkegaard, "Purity of heart is to will one thing."

The essays published in this volume were first presented in 1997 as part of a transatlantic commemoration of the centennial of Drummond's death. In his brief life of slightly more than four and one-half decades, Drummond traveled widely and exerted a remarkable influence on thousands of Christian students, ministers, and missionaries. By the time of his death in 1897, Drummond's essay on I Corinthians 13, *The Greatest Thing in the World*, had become a devotional classic, translated into many languages of the world.

What was the source of Drummond's appeal? The clarity of his writing, the depth of his spirituality, his genius for friendship, his astute scientific mind, his genuine interest in others, his mysterious aloofness, his rare equanimity – he seemed to know neither presumption nor timidity – all of this doubtless contributed to the impression that he was, as Smith put it, "one of the purest, most unselfish, most reverent souls you ever knew." Yet because his life was cut short by a painful bone disease while he was still in his prime, the promise of Drummond as a teacher, scholar, and religious leader was never fulfilled in the way that many of his contemporaries, and perhaps he himself, had once hoped. Drummond seemed for all the world like a man destined for the twentieth century, yet his life ended four years before Queen Victoria died, and nine years before Dietrich Bonhoeffer was born.

In many respects, Drummond's life stands in contrast to that of his great contemporaries. Unlike Moody, he never founded a school. Unlike C. H. Spurgeon, he never presided over a great congregation. There are some parallels between Drummond and David Livingstone, who studied medicine and theology in Glasgow, and who was a writer, scientist, and geographer as well as a missionary. Ten years after Livingstone's death in 1873, Drummond himself set out on a geological exploration of Africa and eventually published a record of these travels in his *Tropical Africa* (1888). Like Livingstone, Drummond was repulsed by the African slave trade and called on the British government to act against it. The essays in this volume offer fresh perspectives on Drummond's life and special aspects of his thought and work which still have an abiding validity more than one hundred years after his death.

On March 14, 1997, New College of the University of Edinburgh, the University of St. Andrews, and Beeson Divinity School of Samford University collaborated in the first phase of a two-part centennial celebration of the legacy of Henry Drummond. This event took place at New College's Martin Hall where

Drummond himself once studied as a divinity student. On this occasion more than one hundred historians, theologians, churchmen, and devotees of the Drummond legacy gathered to discuss the life and work of the great Scottish writer and evangelist. Speakers at this festive commemoration included Professor Alexander C. Cheyne, former principal of New College and Professor Emeritus of Ecclesiastical History in that school; Professor David Bebbington of the University of Stirling; the Very Reverend Professor Robin Barbour, K.C.V.O.; and President Thomas E. Corts of Samford University. Students from St. Andrews University, led by Mr. Eric Motley, helped to coordinate this event recalling Drummond's effective outreach and ministry among university students in his day. Also present for this event were Rev. and Mrs. Finlay Stewart whose original audiovisual presentation on "The Life and Work of Professor Henry Drummond" has been widely shown in churches and civic gatherings in recent years.

The second part of this historic commemoration, sponsored by the same institutions, took place on October 16–17, 1997, on the campus of Samford University in Birmingham, Alabama (U.S.A.). Beeson Divinity School hosted an international symposium on "Henry Drummond In America" which focused on Drummond's significance as a transatlantic evangelical and his role as a personal worker, Christian apologist, and classic interpreter of I Corinthians 13. In addition to scholarly presentations at the symposium, the American festivities also included a banquet at which sculptor Glynn Acree unveiled a life-sized bust of Drummond. A concluding service of worship was held in Beeson Divinity Chapel with greetings offered by the Reverend Richard Buckley, minister of Trinity Possil and Henry Drummond Church in Glasgow, and a sermon by the Very Reverend Dr. Robin Barbour on I Corinthians 13.

The program of the "Henry Drummond In America" events has been included in this volume along with papers presented at both the Edinburgh and Birmingham Drummond symposia. At the Birmingham symposium, Dr. Lewis A. Drummond delivered a lecture entitled "Drummond on Drummond: *The Greatest Thing*

– One Hundred Years Later." Dr. Drummond, a namesake but no direct relation to Henry, is the Billy Graham Professor of Evangelism at Beeson Divinity School. His presentation is not included in this volume since it has appeared as a separate book, *Love, The Greatest Thing in the World* (Grand Rapids: Kregel, 1998).

Alexander C. Cheyne's essay, "The Religious World of Henry Drummond (1851–1897)," locates Drummond in the context of late-Victorian Scottish Presbyterian church life. Earlier in the century, the key figure in this tradition was the redoubtable Thomas Chalmers (d. 1847), a formidable defender of traditional Calvinism whose stand for ecclesiastical autonomy led to the Free Church schism of 1843. Drummond belonged to a new generation of Scottish religious thinkers who, while not repudiating the heritage of the past, attempted to restate it in more contemporary terms, appealing to the heart as well as the mind, to the imagination as well as to reason. Cheyne connects the religious world of Henry Drummond to two major currents of thought in Scottish church life – the rise of historical–critical methodology in the study of the Bible and the influx of an evolutionary model of relating science and religion prompted by the publication of the major writings of Charles Darwin.

Like the famous Old Testament scholar, William Robertson Smith, Drummond was a student of A. B. Davidson from whom he learned to read the Scriptures as the record of God's progressive revelation. Yet Drummond was not unmindful of the potentially destructive effects of biblical criticism and avoided a more radical approach which resulted in "a mutilated Bible." Likewise, Drummond's interest in evolution was combined with a strong evangelical piety and deep devotion to the person of Jesus Christ. In an exchange with Ira D. Sankey near the end of his life, Drummond reaffirmed his long-held beliefs in the cross of Christ, the forgiveness of sins, the hope of immortality based on Christ's resurrection, and the necessity of personal conversion.

In his essay, "Henry Drummond, Evangelicalism and Science," David W. Bebbington examines Drummond's role as a major proponent of the harmonization of Christianity and evolution.

Despite Drummond's restatement of traditional doctrines and theological formulations, his credentials as a card-carrying evangelical were well established by his strong emphasis on conversion and activism. Moreover, as Bebbington points out, his interest in harmonizing science and religion was not entirely out of line with the earlier evangelical tradition. Thomas Chalmers, for example, had published a collection of sermons entitled *Astronomical Discourses* (1817) and later participated in the meeting of the British Association for the Advancement of Science at Cambridge in 1833. Chalmers was the first principal of New College, Edinburgh, but by the time Drummond was a student there the old arguments for natural theology based on the Newtonian worldview were wearing thin. The Darwinian challenge to traditional theism required a new evangelical apologetic. This Drummond supplied in his best-selling book, *Natural Law in the Spiritual World* (1883).

This book was based on lectures Drummond had originally delivered to working men at Possil Park in Glasgow, but its influence reached far beyond that circle and established Drummond as a voice to be reckoned with in the international debates on science and religion. What was the source of Drummond's appeal as a credible evangelical spokesman on this issue? Bebbington answers this question by examining Drummond's role as an evangelist, a scientist, and a romantic.

Clearly, not everyone found Drummond's proposed resolution of this complex set of problems entirely convincing. For example, Bebbington quotes the Free Church theologian James Denney's characterization of *Natural Law* as "a book that no lover of men will call religious, and no student of theology scientific." When Drummond's Lowell Lectures were published in 1894 as *The Ascent of Man* – an intentional riposte to Darwin's famous treatise of 1871 – it elicited even harsher criticisms from both scientists and theologians. Still, despite the fact that Drummond's synthesis has not established itself as a convincing paradigm for later generations, Bebbington is quite right to describe Drummond as "the man of the hour." In retrospect, we can see that Drummond was a courageous pioneer forging a serious evangelical engagement with modern science. Today evangelical critics of Darwin, as well as those who look with greater favor on his legacy, owe a common debt to Henry Drummond for the part he played in opening a conversation which continues still.

Robin S. Barbour's "Henry Drummond, 1851–1897: A Postscript" is a brief but brilliant personal perspective on that winsome character known to his student peers as "the Prince." Barbour grew up hearing family stories about Drummond, including the one about the persuasive powers of his great-grandmother who counseled Drummond to return to college rather than take up full-time evangelistic work with Moody and Sankey. Barbour points to the ultimate motivation behind Drummond's daring scientific achievement and religious work, namely, the glory of God. Drummond was no systematic theologian, but the divine providential ordering of the universe and the Christological basis of human life are evident in all of Drummond's thought. These themes coalesce in a poignant quotation cited by Barbour from one of Drummond's popular Christmas pamphlets: "Though evil stalks the world, it is on the way to execution; though wrong reigns, it must end in self-combustion. The very nature of things is God's Avenger; the very story of civilization is the history of Christ's throne."

Barbour alluded to Drummond's reputation as one of the most effective communicators in his day. Drummond's role as "a professional man of words" is further developed by Thomas E. and Marla Haas Corts in their essay, "'Apples of Gold in Pictures of Silver': Henry Drummond and 'Words Fitly Spoken'." Although he was not formally trained in classical rhetoric, Drummond seems to have possessed a natural intuition for *ethos*, *logos*, and *pathos*, especially the first two, in his speaking and writing. Drawing on contemporary impressions and correspondence as well as published biographies, the Cortses draw an attractive portrait of Drummond, the great communicator. From his early days with Moody and Sankey, Drummond seems to have felt at ease speaking to large gatherings and mass meetings. But while he may have been successful with the crowds, he clearly preferred small group encounters and the one-on-one conversations of the inquiry room.

Drummond never lost sight of the individual. There were many occasions when he was late for a speaking engagement only to be found off in a corner conversing one-on-one with some forlorn young man or serious seeker after Christ.

In addition to reviewing his work as an evangelistic counselor, this essay also examines Drummond's contribution as a teacher, writer, and special friend of children (e.g. his work with the Boys' Brigade) and the more marginal members of the human community. Drummond seems to have had an uncanny capacity for intimacy with others while retaining a sense of reticence and mystery. He was at once charming and reserved, approachable and powerfully attractive, but never inappropriate or too familiar. He was a great stylist and wordsmith, but the appeal of his language was backed up by the authenticity of his life. If the perfect orator is "a good man speaking well," as Quintilian thought, then, in the judgment of his peers, Henry Drummond has reason to be ranked as one of these.

Well before his death in 1897, Drummond's fame had spread far beyond his native Scotland. His writings were translated into many languages of the world, and he was an eagerly sought-after speaker on the international evangelical circuit. Drummond traveled extensively and was well received wherever he went – in France, Germany, Scandinavia, Australia, New Zealand, China, Japan, and Africa. But nowhere was he more keenly welcomed than in North America. President and Mrs. Corts explore the mutual affection between Drummond and the homeland of his friend, D. L. Moody, in their essay, "Henry Drummond: From Scotland to America With Love."

By the late nineteenth century the evangelical movement was led by a loose-knit international cartel of inspirational speakers, missionary statesmen, and parachurch entrepreneurs. In the previous century, John Wesley and George Whitefield had carried the flames of evangelical revival from Great Britain to the American colonies, thus igniting the fires of the First Great Awakening. Moody and Sankey returned the favor in the nineteenth century with successful evangelistic campaigns throughout the British Isles. Drummond's ministry in America was part of this transatlantic evangelical connection which would be further enhanced in the twentieth century through the work of John R. Mott (a major figure in the 1910 Edinburgh Missionary Conference), G. Campbell Morgan, Billy Graham, John R. W. Stott, and others.

The Cortses demonstrate Drummond's growing reputation and influence in America by examining his three extensive visits to the land of Jonathan Edwards and Abraham Lincoln. In 1879 Drummond made an extensive tour of Western North America accompanied by his friend and former teacher, Sir Archibald Geikie. Along the way he conducted an impromptu funeral service for a Colorado miner, visited Moody and Sankey in one of their mid-West campaigns, and spent a week enjoying the cultured society of Boston. His second visit was in 1887 when he returned as the world-renowned author of *Natural Law in the Spiritual World*. This visit involved a whirlwind tour of leading American colleges and universities, Chautauqua speaking engagements, and a presentation on African insects for the American Association for the Advancement of Science.

In 1893 he returned for a final visit. On this trip he delivered the Lowell Lectures, taking the Boston area by storm. He also returned to scenes of earlier triumphs on other campuses in the East and presented a convocation address at the fledgling University of Chicago. At Moody's insistence, he also spoke at the Northfield summer conference even though he had already come under fire for some of his progressive views. In America as in Great Britain, Drummond seemed to be the right man with the right message at the right time. While he never lost the common touch, his impact on college students was phenomenal. He seemed to embody many of the virtues prized by the rising generation of his day – sincerity, decorum, eloquence, manliness, idealism. But his influence transcended the times in which he lived, and his ministry to students bore fruit through the work of the Student Christian Movement, Inter-Varsity Christian Fellowship, and similar organizations.

Robin Barbour's sermon, "'The Greatest of Thing in the World' – Henry Drummond on Love," was presented on October 17, 1997, in the Beeson Divinity Chapel at Samford University.

The service of worship at which this sermon was given also included a reading of Psalm 46, I Corinthians 13, and the singing of Drummond's favorite hymn, "I'm Not Ashamed to Own My Lord." In his sermon Barbour interprets Paul's paean about love in I Corinthians 13 in terms of the person and character of Jesus Christ. This analysis is based on a Trinitarian understanding of God and sees love not as a mere human achievement but rather as a graciously given divine gift – "something that is not within our capacity to produce but only within our capacity to receive."

The essays in this volume have explored various aspects of Drummond's legacy, especially his significance as a religious thinker, evangelical leader, and student minister. But more than one hundred years after his death, he is best remembered as the man who wrote *The Greatest Thing in the World*. Drummond's devotional commentary on I Corinthians 13 was first given as an extemporaneous talk to Christian workers in England when Drummond was persuaded to "fill in" for D. L. Moody at the latter's request. Moody was deeply impressed by what he heard and insisted that Drummond repeat the talk to audiences in America. Once an authorized version began to circulate, Drummond decided to edit the talk for publication. Since then, *The Greatest Thing in the World* has been translated into many languages and widely distributed (see Appendix B).

As the sermon by Robin Barbour intimated, Drummond was not merely expounding the theme of love in general. His thought focuses on the person of Christ. Love, as Drummond describes it, is the fruit of the Holy Spirit. It is also important to remember that Drummond's talk was not originally directed to a general audience but to a group of Christians engaged in evangelical ministry. In the early church the followers of Jesus were known by the kind of love they displayed for one another. The late Francis Schaeffer, whose ministry in some ways paralleled that of Drummond, reminded us of why we ever need to keep coming back to this gospel theme: "Once more let us stress that the end to be attained in working for the purity of the visible church is loving relationship, first to God and then to our brothers. We must not forget that the final end is not what we are against, but what we are for."

The pervasive power of love as the heart of the Christian message was the theme of a special service of worship on February 2, 1958 at the Henry Drummond Parish Church of Scotland in Glasgow. We have included in this volume the order of worship for that service along with the sermon offered by the Reverend C. K. O. Spence. In this sermon he sounds the note of a true Christian ecumenism based on the truth of the gospel and the triumph of God's love in Christ. In his remarkable life and ministry Henry Drummond did much to advance the cause of Christian unity and this, too, is part of the abiding validity of his witness for us today.

TIMOTHY F. GEORGE
Dean of Beeson Divinity School
Samford University
and Senior Editor at *Christianity Today*

Acknowledgements

In January, 1997, my wife and I were in Scotland reflecting upon Henry Drummond and reviewing his papers in the National Library. It was the centennial of his death. As far back as a 1993 sabbatical in Cambridge, we had considered the need for a Drummond commemoration in 1997. But, alas, no such observance was on the horizon.

Seeking relief from a long day of intense library work, we left Glasgow for St. Andrews one drizzly January night to have dinner with a good friend and bright Samford University graduate, Eric Motley, studying on a Rotary Fellowship. We shared with him our disappointment that Drummond's memory was not to be honored in some special way. He was sympathetic, but Drummond was only a name to him and one topic among many before we got the taxi back to Leuchars and the train to our Glasgow hotel.

Within weeks we had an e-mail message from Eric telling us he had contacted officials at St. Andrews and at New College, Edinburgh, who were willing to cooperate in a Henry Drummond event. Out of the genial persistence and personal charm of Eric Motley, the Henry Drummond observance came to pass.

Officials at the National Library of Scotland and at colleges and universities here in America have been extremely helpful. The Reverend and Mrs. Finlay Stewart have been devotees of Drummond for years. The Very Reverend Dr. Robin Barbour was helpful from Eric's first contact, and has come to be a personal friend. He and Mrs. Barbour showed us kind hospitality during an unforgettable day touring Bonskeid, the Barbour ancestral estate, and surround. We had the pleasure of tea with Janet Adam-Smith, daughter of Drummond's devoted friend and biographer, a towering scholar, churchman and public figure in his own right. Lady Aberdeen has graciously entertained us at Haddo House. We owe much to Principal Struther and Mrs. Greta Arnott of St. Andrews University, who have befriended Eric Motley and who early supported the idea of a Drummond event. Dean Duncan Forrester of New College has lent helpful interest. The Reverend C. K. O. Spence, former minister of the Henry Drummond Memorial Church, has shared reminiscences and advice. Bob McCutcheon, who with his wife runs the old bookshop in Stirling, is the community's historian, and has given good counsel.

Drummond was a dear friend to many in his day. As then, so now in retrospect, his life becomes "a perpetual benediction." (D. M. Ross, quoted in Cuthbert Lennox [J. H. Napier], *Henry Drummond: A Biographical Sketch*, 4th ed. [London, 1902], p. 45.)

I am fortunate that Samford University and its Beeson School of Divinity have been willing to be involved in the heritage of Henry Drummond. I owe a great debt to Dean Timothy George and to the Board of Trustees. Sandra L. O'Brien, my assistant and a most capable editor, has efficiently managed the progress toward this volume. Becca Williamson has carried out office detail in her warm and gracious manner. Finally, it was the late Pastor Edward Angel, campus minister of Houghton College (New York), who in the early 1960s gave my wife *The Greatest Thing in the World* when she was an undergraduate. Had it not been for her, as with so many other best parts of my life, I might never have encountered Henry Drummond.

THOMAS E. CORTS
Samford University

Introduction:
Who was Henry Drummond?

Thomas E. Corts

A hundred years have dimmed but not erased memories of Henry Drummond, Scottish evangelist, professor and writer. His remarkable little essay, *The Greatest Thing in the World,* is one of only a few Christian books that have never been out of print in more than 110 years, affirming the judgment of his good friend John Watson (pen name, Ian Maclaren) that "his tract on 'Charity' will long be read, but the man was greater than all his writings." Henry Drummond's books still circulate in the secondhand bookshops of England and America.

A self-confident man of unself-conscious piety, before his lifetime ended at age 45, March 11, 1897, he could be characterized as: (1) a great friend who carefully tended a close circle of friendships, an especially close friend to Dwight L. Moody, the American evangelist; (2) a convincing speaker, with special concern for Christian work among boys and among college students, once called "the greatest leader of young men this century has seen;" (3) a Great Commission-believer, unafraid of modern science, sensitive to common sense issues while thoughtful about personal evangelism; (4) one of the earliest of modern Christian authors to gain and maintain wide popular appeal. For these reasons and more, this modest servant – today most famous as author of *The Greatest Thing in the World* – deserves to be remembered.

On three visits to the United States (1879, 1887, 1893), Henry Drummond was welcomed in colleges and lecture halls. Amherst College granted him an honorary doctorate. At Harvard, he spoke to such crowds of undergraduates that Professor Peabody described his presence "as though a comet had flashed upon the view and had left a trail of light as it sank below the horizon." Of the young Scotsman's visit to Yale, William Lyon Phelps, no stranger to the speaker's rostrum, opined, "I have never seen so deep an impression made on students, by any speaker on any subject."

He also spoke at Chautauqua and gave the Lowell Lectures at Lowell Institute, where in 1893 he had to repeat each lecture in a series, so packed was the hall. An admiring American public dazzled Drummond with offers and opportunities to head colleges, to write for periodicals and to "line his pockets" with the proceeds of the lecture circuit.

Henry Drummond's rise to fame would not have been predicted. His family tree sprouted from deep Christian roots in Stirling, Scotland. His father, also named Henry, had been one of eight sons born to William Drummond, who, in the 1850s, funded a handsome Gothic church and other community beneficence out of his income as head of William Drummond & Sons, prominent seed dealers and nurserymen. Henry, the father, for many years superintended a Sunday School nearby and served on the local school board. Peter Drummond, the father's brother, may be the originator of the modern mass-distributed Gospel tract – eventually leaving the seed business to devote full time to his Stirling Tract Enterprise that dispensed more than 800,000,000 items from its four-storey building in Stirling.

Despite his comfortably prosperous, Christian heritage, Henry Drummond was vocationally a "late-bloomer." From the time of his birth in 1851, the family business was always there, but never held attraction for Henry. His caring family, seeking to provide the best, sent him off to boarding school at age 12. While an acceptable student, he was judged to be "more prominent in the playground than in the class," though he had become aware of his special attraction to science. Later, he remembered feeling an early, nebulous sense of divine call, but not knowing how it would be carried out. Not until his third year in post-university ministry-training and his experience with D. L. Moody did he settle on a future direction – and even that seems subsequently to have been modified.

When barely 15, he matriculated at the University of Edinburgh largely to please his father and was similarly motivated to enter into theological study under the auspices of the Free Church of Scotland. Without feeling a specific call to the ordained ministry, and without intentions to be a minister, he nonetheless passed the church's examination for entrance, the youngest of twenty-five in his class. In leisure moments during student days, he frequented auction houses and bookstalls, enjoyed finding a bargain, and came to appreciate Ruskin, Emerson and George Eliot.

Henry's theological studies were unremarkable until the summer of 1874, before his final year, when the Moody–Sankey campaign came to Scotland. Moody was attracted to the young Scot's Christian spirit, and his sincerity, the very qualities Drummond prized in Moody. With his natural affinity for people, Drummond's effectiveness centered around persons seeking help, individuals who could be personally encouraged and assisted, one-on-one. Moody yielded heavy responsibility to such young shoulders. Despite Drummond's youth and student status, Moody sent him and other ministerial students to help with youth meetings large and small and to follow-up over the succeeding twenty months.

The association with Moody, the demands of preparation for regular speaking, appearing before large audiences – all turned out to be life-defining for the young student. When the Moody campaign was over, after his twenty months of involvement in one of the greatest spiritual awakenings of modern Britain, Henry weighed his father's urging to complete his education against the temptation to leave his studies. He could have followed Moody back to America, or independently tended the revival fires Moody had started in Britain. Even after Drummond had decided and had resumed his theological studies in the fall term of 1875, Moody wrote from the U.S., seeking Henry's help: "I am glad I went to England to learn how to reach young men. Could you come over and help us? We want you much and will see that all expenses are paid. . . . I miss you more than I can tell. You do not know how much I want you with me. Come if you possibly can."

When his course was finished, Henry learned of a faculty death at the Free Church College in Glasgow and with the intercession of friends secured a temporary appointment for the 1877–1878 session as lecturer in Natural Science. As today, not every theological graduate would apply to teach science, but Drummond relied upon a background gained from a number of elective science courses, and his close friendship with Sir Archibald (then, Professor) Geikie, a distinguished geologist. His "temporary" appointment stretched until 1883, a period of time that included his first trip to the United States, a geological exploration around Yellowstone National Park.

In our day, a Natural Science professor seems misplaced in a theological college. However, in the late 1800s, with science not in the standard curricula of Scotland's universities, church leaders still thought that ministers should not be ignorant of God's truth that fits under the rubric of "science."

In 1883, Drummond's life took another important turn as, with a leave of absence from his teaching, he undertook an African expedition. In accordance with the missionary thinking of that day, a group of wealthy Glaswegian Christians was eager to know better the Lake Tanganyika and Nyasaland areas, where it hoped to develop industry and trade, which would help the natives and provide resources for evangelization. In that era, a journey to the African interior was not for the faint of heart, coming only years after David Livingstone had been "lost" and found by Stanley. Drummond was an intelligent choice for the task, having a spirit of adventure, a desire to share the Gospel, and with considerable training in the sciences and geology. His African experience was chronicled in a volume, *Tropical Africa*, published in 1888.

Back from Africa, Drummond might have rested and renewed his strength, but for two factors. First, by April, 1884, Moody was at the peak of another London effort, due to close in June, ending his third mission to Britain. Second, Drummond's book, *Natural Law in the Spiritual World,* had been published just as he had departed for Africa in 1883, and while he was away it had made him something of a celebrity. Forsaking rest and recovery, Drummond went from the ship's dock to participate in the final weeks of Moody's London meetings and to engage in vigorous followup throughout the summer.

His newfound fame trailed publication of *Natural Law in the Spiritual World* in June of 1883. A few clippings and reviews reached Drummond in the wilds of Africa about November, affording him only a long-distance glimmer of the reaction to his book by critics and the public. But by the time he arrived in London, it was a publisher's success. The book, however, with its assertion that "many of the Laws of the Spiritual World, hitherto regarded as occupying an entirely separate province, are simply the Laws of the Natural World" (Preface), incited much interest. To some, the book was the confessed instrument of their conversion to Christ. To others, it was a denial of traditional doctrine. Testimonials on both sides served to make Drummond a much-discussed religious figure, prominent at the early age of 32. Simultaneously both lauded and misunderstood, his motives were at times viciously challenged, and often in print. Yet with the Christian grace that was his "perpetual benediction," he was never heard to say a word against the most violent of his opponents.

Another special opportunity came to Drummond in the winter of 1885. As the anatomy of a revival is ever unknown, its eruption unpredictable, the University of Edinburgh was stirred in December of 1884 by the testimonies of two well-known Cambridge athletes, Stanley Smith and C. T. Studd. Each was as close to a modern sports hero as Britain had known to that time, and each had pledged his life to missionary service in China. The impact of their message to Edinburgh students was profound, but when Smith and Studd had to leave, an organizing committee chose Henry Drummond to carry on with regular Sunday night student meetings. For the task at hand, Drummond was somewhat a "dark horse," but he agreed to speak on a week-to-week basis. Coming from Glasgow every week, his meetings were so successful that they continued for nine years, until his terminal illness forced him to give up. Years afterward, students were commenting on the impact of those student gatherings and it was the unchurch-like meetings that even in America people were eager for Drummond to describe.

In the spring of 1885, yet another unique opportunity came. Through the influence of the Earl and Countess of Aberdeen, a series of three meetings was announced for Sunday nights in April and May in the Ballroom of Grosvenor House, London, the home of the Duke and Duchess of Westminster. Notice of the meetings actually appeared in society columns of the newspapers and crowds of the titled, Members of Parliament, and social elite came to hear Drummond speak in what was surely a most unusual venue. The sessions were well-received and were later tried a second time in June of 1888 – again bringing Drummond into contact with prominent leaders of business and government.

Perhaps it was the attractiveness leaders saw in the young professor during the Grosvenor House meetings that prompted the Liberal Party, under W. E. Gladstone, to attempt to recruit Drummond to stand for Parliament in 1886. After thinking it over, Drummond wrote Gladstone: "I believe that by working in the fixed walk of life which seems to be assigned to me, and which refuses, in spite of private struggles and the persuasion of wisest friends, to release me for this special service, I can do more for every cause of truth and righteousness."

Once described as "the best bewritten man in goody-goodydom," Drummond's greatest publishing success relates to his dear friend, D. L. Moody. When the third crusade ended with a conference for Christians, June 17–19, 1884, Moody and twenty-or-so London crusade workers were invited to regain their strength with a few days' leisure at a supporter's country house outside Tunbridge Wells, southeast of London. Moody, relaxed and enjoying the beautiful Sunday afternoon, William Moody, his father's biographer, states, ". . . succeeded in making a rich discovery for the Christian world . . .". As the group persisted in urging Moody to give an informal devotional, the great evangelist demurred: "No, you've been hearing me for eight months, and I'm quite exhausted. Here's Drummond, he will give us a Bible reading." Somewhat reluctantly, Drummond arose and read I Corinthians 13. Without a note he expounded a message of which Moody said: "It seemed to me that I had never heard anything so beautiful, and I determined not to rest until I brought Henry Drummond to Northfield to deliver that address." Moody wished the message could be read in his Northfield schools once a year and he said "it would be a good thing to have it read once a month in every church 'til it was known by heart." Moody's desire was realized three years later, in 1887, when, visiting Northfield at Moody's special invitation, Drummond presented his message on I Corinthians to the Students Conference and to the August conference.

Besides Moody's insistence, what prompted publication was a desire not to be misquoted. Drummond once explained that he had given his message on Love in an informal setting and later, over dinner at a Swiss hotel, a lady actually handed him a copy of his address in booklet form. As he noted, "I had not intended it for publication, so, in self-defense, I revised it."

In 1887, *The Greatest Thing in the World* was published in America, in a volume recording the messages and sessions of Moody's summer conference for college students, entitled, *A College of Colleges: Led by D. L. Moody*.

By 1889, Drummond determined to publish *The Greatest Thing in the World* as a Christmas volume. It was so well-received that he issued a series of small booklets at Christmas time over the next several years, including, *Pax Vobiscum*, *The Programme of Christianity*, *The Changed Life*, *The City Without A Church*. By February, *The Greatest Thing* had already gone through five editions. Within six months an eager public snatched up 185,000 copies. Drummond never seemed greatly concerned about book royalties, honoraria, or financial matters. (One of the few references to money came in autumn of 1890, when he wrote his mother about some secondhand tea-service, and some china dinnerware that he described as "extravagant purchases" which, he wrote, came from "'The Greatest Thing's' pennies.") When Drummond died in 1897, over 330,000 had been printed in nineteen different languages. Its status as a devotional classic is demonstrated by its record: in more than 110 years, it has *never* been out-of-print, a record claimed by few Christian books and especially books based upon Scripture. While older records are incomplete and the path of publication becomes murky over such a long period of time, it appears that *The Greatest Thing in the World* has sold over 10 million copies in nineteen languages.

Drummond went on to publish still other titles. His work, *The Ascent of Man*, the Lowell Institute Lectures for 1893, was published in May of 1894, an attempt to deal with evolution. While it created considerable controversy in church circles, Drummond never faltered in his commitment to evangelism, ever seeking in his gentlemanly and courtly manner – an approach once described as "the still small voice," after the earthquake and the fire – to represent the cause of Christ.

His great secret seems to have been his exquisite use of the language, his *practical* explanations, presaging the gifted practicality of C. S. Lewis. Drummond once said that most men did not need "to be made wiser, but if there was the chance of helping anyone, a little practically, that was the thing to be done." He focused not on lofty ideology, but on speaking with conviction in a caring, personal way.

Moody said of Henry Drummond:

> No words of mine can better describe his life or character than those in which he has presented to us *The Greatest Thing in the World*. Some men take an occasional journey into the 13th of First Corinthians, but Henry Drummond was a man who lived there constantly, appropriating its blessings and exemplifying its teachings. . . . Never have I known a man who, in my opinion, lived nearer the Master, or sought to do His will more fully.

In 1893, on his last visit to America, word of Drummond's Lowell Lectures on "The Ascent of Man" had reached prominent clergy who knew he was to speak at Moody's Northfield conference. When certain "name" personalities lobbied Moody not to let Drummond speak, fearing him too unorthodox, Moody asked to let him think it over. The next day he told the critics: "I have been shown that he is a better man than I am, and, therefore, he should speak."

At Drummond's funeral in 1897, following a painful two-year illness, Professor Marcus Dods said of Drummond: "Penetrate as deeply as you might into his nature, and scrutinise it as keenly, you never met anything to disappoint, anything to incline you to suspend your judgment or modify your verdict that here you had a man as nearly perfect as you had ever known anyone to be."

In this centennial year of his death, the world can bless the memory of a modest man, who *lived* in I Corinthians 13 and, therefore, could write *The Greatest Thing in the World*.

The Henry Drummond Centenary Symposium

1

❧❧

The religious world of Henry Drummond (1851–1897)

Alexander C. Cheyne

Henry Drummond has never been an easy person to categorize, but it is helpful to remember that – whatever else may be said about him – he was undeniably a Scottish churchman of the late-Victorian period, evincing many of its distinctive characteristics and bound up in many of its peculiar controversies. His entire life, like that of his near contemporary, Robert Louis Stevenson, fell within the second half of the nineteenth century, while his tragically short adult career spanned almost exactly its closing quarter – to be precise, the twenty-five years between his arrival in New College, Edinburgh, as a student of theology in the autumn of 1870 and his illness-enforced departure from the Free Church College in Glasgow (where he had taught for the best part of two decades) in the spring of 1895.

During that brief but tumultuous period, Scottish Presbyterianism's theological complexion changed more rapidly and profoundly than at perhaps any other time between the Reformation and our own day. The Free Church, in particular, in which Drummond had been brought up, and whose servant he became, quite suddenly surrendered its cherished early reputation as one of the most staunchly conservative and traditionalist bodies in Christendom – deeply committed to the scholastic Calvinism of the Westminster Confession of Faith, ardently proclaiming its belief in Holy Scripture as "the *unerring* standard of the Word of God," strongly Sabbatarian, wary alike of liturgical, homiletic, and social innovations, and proud of its universally acknowledged position within the mainstream of evangelical faith and life. Instead, it joined its sister churches in Scotland in an extensive and fundamental refashioning of religion as it had been known to John Knox and his associates, to the Covenanters, and even to a high proportion of church folk in the generations between William Carstares and Thomas Chalmers.

Drummond himself was by no means an initiator of the changes just mentioned. In most of them he was not even a prominent figure. But such was his almost uncanny sensitivity to the intellectual and spiritual currents of the day that his attitudes and utterances frequently mirrored the central concerns and convictions that were reshaping belief and conduct in the years when Gladstone dominated the political scene, when Huxley and Spencer carried the banner of Darwinian science, and when Protestants north of the Anglo-Scottish Border looked for leadership to such magisterial figures as Robert Rainy (in the Free Church), John Cairns (in the United Presbyterian Church), and the redoubtable Auld Kirk triumvirate of John Tulloch in St. Andrews, John Caird in Glasgow, and Archibald Hamilton Charteris in Edinburgh.

A more questioning, less serenely satisfied, attitude to credal and confessional statements in general, and to the Westminster Confession in particular, was one aspect of Victorian Scotland's religious revolution which found a voice in Henry Drummond.

As late as 1865, Principal Robert Candlish of New College may well have spoken for most Scottish Presbyterians when he referred to the Westminster "Standards" (the Confession and the Catechisms) as "the only safe anchorage in any and every storm;"[1] and certainly all ministers, whether Free, United Presbyterian or Established, were still required at ordination to profess their unreserved adherence to the faith as formulated in the 1640s. But in the very year of Candlish's pronouncement, Principal Tulloch

---

[1] R. S. Candlish, *The Fatherhood of God*, 2nd ed. (1865), p. 289.

of St. Andrews sounded a very different note. Rejecting what he called "the popular ecclesiastical notion of creeds and confessions as *credenda* to be accepted very much as we accept the statements of Scripture itself," he went on to assert that "those creeds and confessions are neither more nor less than the intellectual labours of great and good men assembled for the most part in synods and councils, all of which, as our Confession itself declares, 'may err, and many have erred.' They are stamped with the infirmities no less than the nobleness of the men who made them."[2] By Drummond's time, the view of Tulloch and others similarly minded had gained the upper hand in all three Presbyterian bodies in Scotland. In 1879, the United Presbyterian Church redefined its relationship to the Confession, its "principal subordinate standard," allowing ministers and office-bearers some freedom in their inter-pretation of it. In 1892, the Free Church followed suit with another Declaratory Act, and the Church of Scotland behaved similarly at the first available opportunity (in 1910). The old exclusiveness – and possibly the old precision and consistency – of Reformed theology was relegated to the past; suspicion of "dogmatism" and the elevation of life over doctrine were in the ascendant.

Drummond's wholehearted sympathy with the new mood cannot be doubted. "There is," he once observed, "no more un-fortunate word in our Church's vocabulary than 'Standard.' A Standard is a thing that stands. Theology is a thing that moves."[3] Of traditional Reformed doctrine he remarked, "We too can still preach it, but to some of us it has a hollow sound. If we could confess the honest truth, our words for it are rather those of respect than of enthusiasm: We read it, hear it, study it, and preach it, but can hardly say it kindles or moves us."[4] Going even further, he accused it of offering the world an unChristianized God whose outstanding characteristics were anger and vengeance, of laying

---

[2] J. Tulloch, "Theological Controversy" (An address delivered to the Theological Society in the University of Edinburgh) (Edinburgh, 1865), pp. 26–27.

[3] H. Drummond, *The New Evangelism and Other Papers*, 2nd ed. (London, 1899), p. 7.

[4] Ibid., pp. 10–11.

all the emphasis on the believer's status rather than his character, and of giving the impression that salvation was "a thing that came into force at death" instead of being "a thing for life."[5] (There are echoes in this of famous sermons by Caird on "The Comparative Influence of Character and Doctrine" and by Tulloch on "Religion and Theology.")

The threatened decline of vital religion in British society was, Drummond believed, at least partly due to the propositional theology of the outgoing age, "tied up in neat parcels, systematised and arranged in logical order," whereas for him biblical truth was "a fountain." Above all, he desired – in the spirit of Horace Bushnell (and perhaps George Macdonald) – to have preachers appeal not so much to the reason as to the imagination. "God's truth," he contended, "will not go into a word. You must put it in an image." Indeed, the new evangelism of his dreams

> will never say that it sees quite clearly. It may remain ignorant, but it will never presume to say there is no darkness, no mystery, no unknown. . . . It is not all clear as the old theology; it has the dimness of an older theology which sees through a glass darkly, which knows in part, and which, because it knows in part, knows the more certainly that it shall know hereafter.[6]

(One might add that for Drummond religious truth was in the final analysis communicated not through propositions but through *persons* – a conviction which he made good in innumerable instances by the almost numinous quality of his own deeply impressive character.)

Another aspect of Victorian Scotland's religious revolution may be seen in the application to biblical study of the principles and methods of literary and historical criticism. Effected by the same influences which had helped to erode the impregnability of Westminster Calvinism, this momentous development was pioneered – or at least made respectable – in Drummond's part of the world by his Old Testament teacher at New College, the ever-

---

[5] Ibid., p. 18.
[6] Ibid., pp. 23–33.

memorable Andrew Bruce Davidson. As a result of Davidson's labours (which were, of course, anticipated or paralleled or carried further by numerous other scholars in Britain, Europe, and North America), students of Holy Writ learned to read it with the aid of historical rather than dogmatic spectacles, to pay as much attention to the original context of its pronouncements as to their later significance, and to recognize that even the most sublime topics had been handled by human – and therefore fallible – intermediaries. They were also encouraged as exegetes to follow the good example of those sixteenth-century reformers who had deferred less to ecclesiastical tradition and time-honoured dogmatic formularies than to what in their considered opinion the text of Scripture actually said.

The implications for the ordinary believer of this cataclysmic change have been described by one particularly discerning commentator as follows:

> It was . . . as if the piety of the Church had habitually been meeting with its Divine Friend in confidence and comfort within the same familiar house; but one day found the place invaded by architects and builders who were partly demolishing it, wholly rearranging it, and making it seem new and strange in every room. Even though they asserted that these changes were merely external and that the One formerly met with was still there, still the whole *genius loci* seemed affected by the new conditions.[7]

What the same writer described as "a panic of consternation and a storm of controversy" naturally accompanied the critical movement: it reached its climax in 1881 with the deposition of Davidson's star pupil, William Robertson Smith, from his Old Testament Chair at Aberdeen for what was described as "a singular and culpable lack of sympathy with the reasonable anxieties of the Church as to the bearing of critical speculations on the integrity and authority of Scripture."[8]

[7] P. C. Simpson, *The Life of Principal Rainy* (London, 1909), Vol. I, pp. 312–313.

[8] J. S. Black and G. W. Chrystal, *The Life of William Robertson Smith* (London, 1912), p. 425.

Drummond, however, seems to have had very little difficulty in adapting to the new situation. Though I have come across no record of the impression made upon him by Davidson's lectures, it is difficult to think of his being unmoved by their combination of meticulously careful scholarship, spiritual, and psychological insight and restrained if sometimes almost shattering eloquence. We know for a fact that he was among those who deplored Professor Smith's deposition, and that he was a lifelong friend and admirer of Marcus Dods, to whose congregation in Glasgow he belonged and whose controversial candidature for the New Testament Chair at Edinburgh he warmly supported. He was also – and this can hardly have been without effect – a teaching colleague in the Free Church College at Glasgow of Smith's faithful defender, Professor J. S. Candlish, of the *avant garde* Professor A. B. Bruce (subject, with Dods, of a heresy trial in 1890) and, during the mid-1890s, of his own future biographer, Professor George Adam Smith, who was himself to be accused of heresy in the early years of the present century.

We, therefore, find him (in, for example, an article on "The Contribution of Science to Christianity," which appeared in *Expositor* in 1885) speaking of the "Bible in two forms" that confronted modern man. "The one is the Bible as it was presented to our forefathers; the other is the Bible of modern theology." His preference, clearly, was for the latter, and although he made no secret of his indebtedness to what he called "the development theory" of evolutionary science, it is also clear that he had absorbed the teaching of biblical scholars like Davidson, Robertson Smith, and Dods.

> The Bible [he averred] is not a book which has been made; . . . it has grown. . . . It is not an even plane of proof text without proportion or emphasis, or light and shade; but a revelation varied as nature, with the Divine in its hidden parts, in its spirit, its tendencies, its obscurities, and its omissions. . . . It is a record of inspired deed as well as of inspired words, an ascending series of inspired facts in a matrix of human history.

Again, he was anxious to point out that the revolution in biblical studies had not been destructive, nor was the transformed book "a mutilated Bible:" the main warrant for what had taken place was to be found in Holy Scripture itself. And he summed up his attitude – very characteristically – as follows:

> Instead . . . of reading all our theology into Genesis, we see only the alphabet there. In the later books, we see primers – first, second, and third: the truths stated provisionally as for children, but gaining volume and clearness as the world gets older. Centuries and centuries pass, and the mind of the disciplined race is at last deemed ripe enough to receive New Testament truth, and the revelation culminates in the person of Christ.[9]

Various other aspects of late-Victorian thought and life found either a moving spirit or an exemplar in Henry Drummond; but no study, however cursory, can avoid mentioning two movements in which he was deeply involved and from which his fame was in large measure derived. These were, of course, the Darwinian revolution in science and the Evangelical revivalism associated with the names of Moody and Sankey.

Darwin's epoch-making treatises were both published in the years immediately before Drummond entered on his life's work: *The Origin of Species* in 1859 and *The Descent of Man* in 1871. Together, they raised profound questions for Christian theology – not least its doctrines of man, of creation, of providence and of Scripture – and created divisions within the Christian camp which the passage of time has only partially overcome. According to one modern authority, at least three distinct responses were made by the churches to the Darwinian challenge: the traditionalist, which preserved classical doctrines with little modification, the modernist, which sought to reformulate the faith in the light of the new knowledge, and the liberal (a mean, as it were, between more extreme positions), which agreed with modernism in welcoming the scientific evidence for evolution but held that too great a departure had been made from traditional views of God and man.[10] If we must use such terminology, it is clear that Drummond stood

---

[9] Drummond, *New Evangelism*, pp. 177–183.

[10] I. G. Barbour, *Issues in Science and Religion* (New York, 1968), p. 365 and elsewhere.

among the "modernists," whose entire understanding of things was dominated by the concept of evolution – though we should remember that in his case the dominance of evolution was combined with deep devotion to the person of Jesus Christ.

The two volumes which publicized Drummond's views in Britain, on the Continent of Europe, and in North America – *Natural Law in the Spiritual World* (1883) and *The Ascent of Man* (1894) – were bestsellers in their day; but they have not worn very well. Even at the time, percipient critics like the young theologian James Denney drew attention to basic flaws in the earlier work, describing it as "a book which no lover of men will call religious, and no student of theology scientific;"[11] while the fullest recent history of the period – Drummond and Bulloch's *The Church in Late Victorian Scotland* – remarks, devastatingly, that Drummond was "essentially an amateur and a dilettante, of no importance as scientist or theologian. His academic qualifications were of the slightest, and his great gifts lay in communication."[12] It is true, of course, that distinguished scientists like Professor Balfour Stewart and Professor P. G. Tait (authors of *The Unseen Universe* of 1875, to which Drummond was greatly indebted) and Professor Archibald Geikie, the pioneer geologist, were much more favorable, but it can be objected that they were all personal friends. In our time, too, the eminent historian of science, Dr. Joseph Needham, declared in his *Time: The Refreshing River* (1943) that "*Natural Law in the Spiritual World* is a naive work, but it has the naivete of something fundamentally true," and even gave it as his verdict that "when all criticisms have been made, *Natural Law in the Spiritual World* remains a great book."[13] As a Marxist, however (though also an Anglo-Catholic), Needham might perhaps be expected to welcome Drummond's identification of spiritual and natural laws, and in any case the general weight of scholarly opinion seems to point in another direction. Without anticipating the final judgment of

[11] J. Moffatt, ed., *Letters of Principal James Denney to His Family and Friends* (London, 1922), p. 11.
[12] A. L. Drummond and J. Bulloch, *The Church in Late Victorian Scotland 1874–1900* (Edinburgh, 1978), p. 26.
[13] J. Needham, *Time: The Refreshing River* (London, 1943), p. 29.

history, it must be admitted that most present-day authorities are unimpressed by what they see as Drummond's regrettable subservience to the "social Darwinism" of Herbert Spencer, find his application of biological concepts to the spiritual realm generally unconvincing and look with disfavour on what Dr. J. R. Moore has discerningly described as "the naturalisation of the spiritual world."[14]

What verdict then are we to pass on this facet of Drummond's career? Without straying into fields of continuing controversy, three comments would seem to be in order. Firstly, whatever our view of Drummond's principal thesis, at least we may credit him with homing in upon topics of primary importance and appealing to the often unspoken interests and questionings of a large section – untrained but nevertheless concerned – of the general public. As Professor Owen Chadwick pointed out in his Gifford Lectures on *The Secularisation of the European Mind in the Nineteenth Century*, perhaps a popular book upon a theme among the most profound and difficult known to man is rather a symbol, the focus of the inarticulate longings of a decade, than an instructless like a book of elementary physics, and if so, its influence might be seen in its focusing and not in its instruction; articulating an attitude towards life which some people wanted to articulate and could not articulate for themselves or did not like to articulate for themselves.[15] In other words, *Natural Law in the Spiritual World* and *The Ascent of Man* are important chiefly because their author knew what chiefly mattered to numerous thinking people in the 1880s and 1890s, what they wanted to think about even more than what they thought. Like a highly sensitive anemometer, Drummond helps us to measure the intellectual wind pressure of his day.

Secondly, we should be able to welcome the positive attitude to natural science which Drummond adopted at a time when many Christian believers found antagonism only too easy. There is, for

[14] J. R. Moore, "Evangelicals and Evolution: Henry Drummond, Herbert Spencer, and the Naturalisation of the Spiritual World," *Scottish Journal of Theology* 38 (1985): 383–417.

[15] O. Chadwick, *The Secularisation of the European Mind in the Nineteenth Century* (Cambridge, 1975), p. 172.

example, something disarmingly attractive about assertions such as this (from his article on "The Contribution of Science to Christianity").

> Religion is probably only learning for the first time how to approach science. Their former intercourse, from faults on both sides, and these mainly due to juvenility, is not a thing to remember. After the first quarrel – for they began the centuries hand-in-hand – the question of religion to science was simply, "How dare you speak at all?" Then as science held to its right to speak just a little, the question became, "What new menace to our creed does your latest discovery portray?" But, we do not speak now of the right to be heard, or of menaces to our faith, or even of compromises. Our question is a much maturer one – we ask what *contribution* science has to bestow, what good gift the wise men are bringing now to lay at the feet of our Christ.[16]

Thirdly, even Drummond's denigrators are prepared to concede that – wrong-headed though he may have been in many particulars – he nevertheless did something to lessen the estrangement between science and religion in the age of Huxley and Tyndall. Professor Colin Russell of the Open University speaks for quite a number of conservative evangelicals when he contends that "Drummond could elevate evolution to a cosmic principle (which he then Christianised) precisely because he sat so lightly to the biblical doctrines which, in other men, restrained and modified their allegiance to any principle of universal progress." But, at the same time he allows that those who, like Drummond, attempted a synthesis between biblical and evolutionary thought deserve credit for (in Russell's phrase) "bridging these troubled waters" and diminishing the baneful tumult between science and religion.[17] It is an important concession, and one which we may believe Drummond himself would have appreciated.

Despite all that has been said so far, it was almost certainly as a missionary preacher that Drummond did his best work. The

[16] Drummond, *New Evangelism*, p. 155.

[17] C. A. Russell, *Cross-currents: Interactions between Science and Faith* (Leicester, 1985), pp. 162, 165.

nineteenth century was very much a century of "revivals": from the activities of the Haldanes at its beginning, through William Burns and Robert Murray McCheyne in the pre-Disruption years to the great (predominantly layman-led) movement of 1859 and the mass evangelism of a host of transatlantic missioners in its final quarter. It was in the company of two of the latter – Dwight L. Moody and Ira D. Sankey – that Drummond really found his vocation; but in his hands evangelism and revivalism became rather different from anything that had previously been known in Scotland. The essential content of his preaching may have been the same as that of all his predecessors (though he struck a new note, as we have seen, in what he had to say about both Scripture and the Confession), but the methods by which he communicated his message displayed an unprecedented sensitivity to the individual needs of his hearers, while the message itself was altogether kindlier, less minatory and more exclusively concerned with Jesus Christ as the embodiment of the saving love of God than that which had long distinguished revivalistic preaching in Scotland.

Galvanized into action during Moody's first and most effective Scottish campaign between 1873 and 1875, and proving himself equally at home with large crowds and with individuals in the inquiry room, he displayed from the outset a unique command of oratory and counseling skills. Working men in the Possil Park district of Glasgow, gentry and nobility at Grosvenor House (the Duke of Westminster's residence) in London, the lads of the newly created Boys' Brigade, young men of the Y.M.C.A. and – above all – student gatherings in Britain, North America, Australia, and the Continent of Europe: all acknowledged his well-nigh mesmeric persuasiveness and charm.

Nowhere was he more effective than in Edinburgh's Oddfellows Hall, where for the last ten years or so of his life every winter weekend found him addressing hundreds of students (medical men in particular) on central topics of the Faith, under the benevolent patronage of eminent academics from various university departments. The cost to Drummond was considerable, but the admiring account given by his biographer, George Adam Smith, suggests that the results were more than commensurate with the time and energy expended.

> He shut himself off [writes Smith] from the pulpits of his Church, denied his friends, turned from the public, banished reports, and endured infinite misrepresentation, if only he might make sure of the students. . . . And measured by results, almost everything [else] he did seems less; for the field was one on which other ministers of religion had many failures, and he conspicuously succeeded. Hundreds of men who never went to church were won for Christ at his meetings. He invented methods that are now employed wherever students join for religious service. He preached the Gospel of Christ with a fullness and with a pertinacity of personal application which he never excelled on any other platform. And so, he influenced thousands of lives, which are now [1898] at work among many nations, in all those professions of governing and teaching to which the University is a necessary introduction.[18]

All, it seems, was unpretentious and straightforward, with an avoidance of clerical or theological catch-phrase, ponderously literary forms of expression, and high-pressure religious sales talk. To quote Smith's biography again: "There is no sensation in the addresses, nor any imposition of authority; no artificiality or false mysticism; but the style is as simple as the thinking; it is one sensible man talking to others of his own generation."[19] And, of course, the central, overarching theme (as in most liberal evangelical preaching at that time) was not the Church, nor the fallenness of humanity, nor even the biblical "scheme of salvation," but Jesus Christ. According to his biographer's testimony, "He (Jesus Christ) was for him the source of all life and light; the assurance of the forgiveness of sins; the daily nourishment of the soul; the one power sufficient for a noble life; the solution of all problems; the motive and example of all service."[20] It is surely no coincidence that out of all Drummond's many addresses the one which has

[18] George Adam Smith, *The Life of Henry Drummond*, 2nd ed. (London, 1899), pp. 294–295.

[19] Ibid., p. 326.

[20] Ibid.

worn best and best represents the heart of his message is that model sermon on I Corinthians 13: *The Greatest Thing in the World.*

Needless to say, there were criticisms, as when he was accused of preaching a lamentably one-sided Gospel and (in particular) of playing down the centrality of the Atonement in the proclamation of Christian truth. Part of his answer appears in what he wrote to an anxious relative on the subject. "Of course," he replied, "you may think I make an error of judgment in my reading of the popular pulse, and in not writing books about the fundamentals. But there seem to me many more books on those aspects of Christ's work than the others, and I must give the message that, *in addition*, seems to me to be needed."[21] His most effective retort, however, is to be found in a brief exchange of letters with his old associate, Sankey, as late as 1892. The American quoted some phrases, attributed to Drummond, which ran as follows:

> The power to set the heart right, to renew the springs of action, comes from Christ. The sense of the infinite worth of the single soul, and the recoverableness of a man at his worst, are the gifts of Christ. The freedom from guilt, the forgiveness of sins, come from Christ's cross; the hope of immortality springs from Christ's grave. Personal conversion means for life a personal religion, a personal trust in God, a personal debt to Christ, a personal dedication to His cause.

Were these, Sankey asked, indeed Drummond's words? Did he stand by them still? Back came the unequivocal reply: "These *are* my words, and there has never been an hour when the thoughts which they represent were not among my deepest convictions."[22] If there was anything new in Drummond's message, it consisted partly in a shift of emphasis and partly in the impact of his own remarkable character and personality.

That personality was his supreme gift to the Christian cause. He had his detractors, naturally; but quite a few who began by being suspicious of him were eventually conquered – or almost conquered – by one whom today's world would no doubt describe

[21] Ibid., p. 411.
[22] Ibid., pp. 7–8, 412–413.

as "charismatic." In 1886, the great panjandrum of religious journalism, William Robertson Nicoll, said about him: "I cannot believe that all that evangelising, banqueting, reconciling, and philandering can ever be the material of a sincere and healthy life."[23] Two years later, though referring rather off-takingly to Drummond's well-known sartorial elegance – "He has a Sapphire Blue Velvet waistcoat like the Body of Heaven in its clearness" – Nicoll had begun to surrender: "What he said was excellent, and his manner was even better than his matter – both manly and modest – just the right thing."[24] And by 1897, we find him expressing penitence for earlier criticisms.

> Of course, [he wrote] I was sensible of the peculiar spell Henry Drummond always had, a spell that fascinated some, and in others excited an unaccountable feeling, not in the least of repulsion, but of resentment. One felt as if an advantage were being taken of his mind by a power not of the nature of reason and was irritated by it. . . . I am sorry now when I think of it, for Drummond was the most generous and gentle of men, and it must have been to him inexplicably and gratuitously rude.[25]

Theological conservatives never abandoned their suspicion (unless they were as generous as Moody); but it was not Drummond the man but his ideas that they found distasteful. In personal encounter, he captivated most people. "One did not realise," wrote John Watson (Ian Maclaren), "how commonplace and colourless other men were till they stood side by side with Drummond. . . . [He was] the most vital man I ever saw, who never loitered, never wearied, never was conventional, pedantic, formal, who simply revelled in the fullness of life."[26] Professor Geikie, whose favorite pupil Drummond was, averred that he had "never met with a

[23] T. H. Darlow, *William Robertson Nicoll: Life and Letters* (London, 1925), p. 70.
[24] Ibid., p. 87.
[25] Ibid., p. 155.
[26] H. Drummond, *The Ideal Life and Other Unpublished Addresses with Memorial Sketches by Ian Maclaren [pseud] and W. Robertson Nicoll*, 3rd ed. (London, 1899), pp. 26, 28.

man in whom transparent integrity, high moral purpose, sweetness of disposition, and exuberant helpfulness were more happily combined with wide culture, poetic imagination, and scientific sympathies than they were in Henry Drummond."[27] Equal admiration was shown by Professor Carnegie Simpson in his biography of Principal Rainy, where he remarked that although Drummond passed through two of the severest ordeals that can befall anyone – immense popularity and intense pain – neither succeeded in changing him from "the natural and unselfish and pure soul he had always been;"[28] and George Adam Smith (who made the same point at the beginning of his study) quotes the striking if characteristic testimonial of D. L. Moody that "Some men take an occasional journey into the 13th of First Corinthians, but Henry Drummond was a man who lived there constantly, appropriating its blessings and exemplifying its teachings."[29]

More than half a century after Drummond's tragically early death, Principal David Cairns of Aberdeen paid him one of the most memorable tributes of all – a tribute which perhaps brings out more clearly than any other both the personal charm and the theological importance of Henry Drummond.

> I am sure [wrote Cairns] that *for his audiences* Drummond's methods were much better [than Moody's]. He understood us, for he had singular intuitive gifts, and knew that many of us students were honestly groping our way, in a very troubled period of thought, to further light. . . . Not that he was either a theologian or a philosopher. He was neither to any considerable extent. But, there is an inner region, in religious as in moral matters, in which faith and ideals have their birth. Theologies and philosophies formulate and attack or defend these. But, they cannot create them. The pure or penitent in heart see God, and then they think about Him, and theologies and philosophies are the result. In the inner sphere Drummond had a good deal to say to us. . . . When he died . . . still in his prime, I felt as if I had lost a dear friend. I still remember the day, with its whirling snow. . . . I am certainly thankful to have had him as one

[27] Smith, *Drummond*, pp. 9–10.
[28] Simpson, *Rainy*, Vol. II, p. 170.
[29] Smith, *Drummond*, p. 8.

of my leaders in spiritual things, for he helped me greatly in a transition time at once to hold fast to what was permanent in the old tradition and at the same time to go on into the new world of thought with a new freedom.[30]

---

[30] D. S. Cairns, *David Cairns: An Autobiography*, ed. D. Cairns and A. H. Cairns (London, 1950), pp. 113–117.

2

Henry Drummond, evangelicalism and science

David W. Bebbington

Henry Drummond (1851–1897) was a prominent figure in the late-Victorian evangelical world. In his day evangelicalism formed the mainstream of nearly all the Protestant denominations in the British Isles, certainly embracing Drummond's Free Church of Scotland. The movement typically placed emphasis on conversion and activism, and Drummond shared these preoccupations. Conversion is the central theme of his most celebrated work *Natural Law in the Spiritual World* (1883). The natural man, he contended, is dead until he receives life from God. Likewise, the call to conversion was urgent even in Drummond's addresses to London high society, organized by Lord and Lady Aberdeen in the gilded ballroom of Grosvenor House during the spring of 1885.[1] Flowing from conversion was activism, an intense commitment to evangelistic and social work. After a week's lectures in Glasgow, Drummond would habitually return to Edinburgh for the weekend. His purpose was not to rest but to exhort a different set of students. In his writings he flays the laziness of ministers who, in order to preach, do no more than take down from their shelves their volumes of theology.[2] Instead, they need to be active beyond the pulpit. In

[1] George Adam Smith, *The Life of Henry Drummond*, 2nd ed. (London, 1899), pp. 253–258.

[2] H. Drummond, *The New Evangelism and Other Papers*, 2nd ed. (London, 1899), p. 24.

an address on "The Three Elements of a Complete Life," he identified two elements as God and Love: the third is Work.[3] Conversion and activism were as much the hallmarks of Drummond's career as they were of the evangelical movement in any age.

There is more room for doubt about whether he shared the movement's other two most salient characteristics, devotion to the Bible and to the cross. Drummond's addresses contain passages where he appears to deprecate biblicism. "I believe in Christianity," he told an audience of young men in America, ". . . not because I believe in this book. I believe in this book because I believe in Christianity."[4] He composed no systematic expositions of the Scriptures and accepted biblical criticism without reserve. Yet, Drummond was preoccupied with the Bible. At one point in the argument of *Natural Law in the Spiritual World,* the foot of the page is peppered with footnotes designed to vindicate the scientific prescience of the New Testament.[5] One of his posthumously published papers was entitled "The Evolution of Bible Study." Its aim is to establish the hermeneutic principle that the Bible never reveals anything which human beings could discover for themselves.[6] If that position limits biblical authority in the sphere of science, its object is to entrench the status of the Bible as a medium of revelation. The old view of inspiration, he told the members of the Theological Society at the Free Church College, Glasgow, was now untenable, but the study of the inward character of its component books had restored the Bible to them.[7] The idea has an autobiographical ring. It seems that Drummond, though living through the critical reappraisal of the Scriptures in the last quarter of the nineteenth century, emerged with a renewed zest for the Bible much like that of his friend and biographer, the biblical scholar George Adam Smith. He had come to believe in progressive

---

[3] H. Drummond, *Stones Rolled Away and Other Addresses to Young Men Delivered in America* (London, 1903), p. 184.

[4] Drummond, *Stones Rolled Away*, p. 111.

[5] H. Drummond, *Natural Law in the Spiritual World,* 19th ed. (London, 1887), p. 296.

[6] H. Drummond, *The Evolution of Bible Study* (New York, 1901), p. 22.

[7] Drummond, *New Evangelism*, pp. 53–54.

revelation, an understanding which, he held, made the Bible "as impregnable as nature."[8]

In a similar way Drummond reformulated the doctrine of the atonement. Teaching about the significance of the crucifixion of Christ is much less prominent in Drummond's pages than in the writings of most contemporary evangelicals, and the more conservative among them criticized him on this score. On occasion, he was willing to decry the whole doctrine.[9] Yet his purpose, as he makes plain in *Natural Law*, was not to turn attention away from the atonement but to warn against its perversion. It was vain, he explained, to suppose that a person was saved merely through knowing that Christ died for sinners. The doctrine might have "no more vital contact with the soul than the priest or sacrament, no further influence on life and character than stone and lime."[10] Empty words about the cross would not bring about authentic conversions. When rightly understood, however, the atonement did have power. Drummond held that new life had to be breathed into the doctrine. Thinking minds, he believed, were turning away from it because in its traditional form, it was seen as inhuman, the vindictive killing of a son by his father. Drummond, therefore, reinterpreted the atonement as "the professed meaning and omnipotent dynamic of the law of sacrifice."[11] The ethical principle of sacrifice ran through the universe: the death of Christ was its supreme example. Drummond was producing a version of the moral influence theory of the atonement. That was unusual among evangelicals, but its author had no doubt that he was restoring the "central doctrine to theology."[12] He wanted to be not less, but more, loyal to the atonement. Despite the smaller stress in his teaching on the cross, as on the Bible, Drummond wished to remain within the evangelical movement, if necessary by stretching its boundaries.

[8] Quoted by Smith, *Drummond*, p. 237.
[9] Drummond, *New Evangelism*, p. 27.
[10] Drummond, *Natural Law*, p. 331.
[11] Drummond, *New Evangelism*, p. 58.
[12] Ibid., p. 56.

He certainly possessed typical evangelical attitudes. The movement, which had secured the abolition of the slave trade in 1807, remained deeply hostile to slavery. Drummond detested the institution. In 1883, he followed in the steps of David Livingstone to the African interior, five years later publishing an account of his journey in *Tropical Africa*. In the preface he denounces the slave trade as "the open sore of the world." Arab merchants, he explains, enslaved carriers to take ivory to the coast, and so he advocates a drastic solution: "the sooner the last elephant falls before the hunter's bullet the better for Africa."[13] The extermination of the elephant would mark a stage in closing down the slave trade. British ascendancy, furthermore, was essential in the region if it was to be saved from the curse of slavery. Drummond's book was one of the precipitants of the British declaration of a protectorate over Nyasaland – the later Malawi – in 1891. The passionate commitment to the anti-slavery cause marked Drummond as an heir of the evangelical tradition.

The evangelical movement as a whole is commonly supposed to have been hostile to science. During the nineteenth century, it is thought, its biblicism set the movement in opposition to the advance of science. Fresh discoveries showed that the world was much older than the Bible seemed to teach. There were apparently contradictions between Genesis and geology. Furthermore, pre-occupation with the natural world might look to evangelicals like a waste of time, a diversion from the priorities of the gospel. Thus, there were protests from Scottish congregations when ministers preached about the work of God in creation because the theme seemed remote from his work in salvation, the proper subject for the pulpit.[14] So, undoubtedly, there were tensions between evangelicalism and science. Nevertheless, the prevailing mood among evangelicals during the first half of the nineteenth century, the period before Drummond's birth in 1851, assumed a harmony between science and religion. Thomas Chalmers, the leader of the Free Church and first principal of New College, Edinburgh,

---

[13] H. Drummond, *Tropical Africa* (London, 1888), p. 20.
[14] T. Dick, *The Christian Philosopher* (Glasgow, 1846), Vol. I, p. 26.

enthusiastically attended an early meeting of the British Association for the Advancement of Science at Cambridge in 1833.[15] Round Chalmers, there was a distinguished circle who combined evangelical theology with scientific practice: Sir David Brewster, a specialist in optics and eventually principal of the University of Edinburgh; John Fleming, Professor of Natural History at King's College, Aberdeen; and Hugh Miller, the ex-stonemason who popularized geological investigation. Paul Baxter has shown in a doctoral dissertation on this group, that evangelicalism and science meshed closely together in their minds.[16] They confronted intellectual problems, but equally they proposed satisfying solutions. The newly appreciated length of geological time, for example, was ingeniously reconciled with the first chapter of Genesis. A vast interval, according to Chalmers, may have elapsed between the creation of all things described in verse one and the ordering of the universe expounded from verse two. Alternatively, according to Miller, the six days of creation could be interpreted figuratively as long epochs of time.[17] Either scheme of harmonization seemed to uphold the integrity of geology as much as of Scripture. Science and religion were understood as part of the same divine world order.

How was this synthesis of knowledge possible? The explanation lies in the Enlightenment premises adopted by evangelical thinkers. They, as much as their contemporaries, pursued the scientific investigation of the world within an intellectual framework associated with the age of reason. Sir Isaac Newton, whose laws shed light in dark places, was their model. They exalted the method of induction, calling their own brand of Christianity "experimental religion." Thomas Chalmers' most famous sermons, the *Astronomical Discourses* (1817), praised Newton and gloried in the triumphs of the rational investigation of the

---

[15] W. Hanna, ed., *Memoirs of the Life and Writings of Thomas Chalmers, D.D., LL.D.* (Edinburgh, 1849–1852), Vol. III, pp. 380–384.

[16] Paul Baxter, "Science and Belief in Scotland, 1805–1868: The Scottish Evangelicals" (Ph.D. dissertation, University of Edinburgh, 1985).

[17] Ibid., pp. 71–72, 139–140.

heavens.[18] "Nothing," he wrote in 1814, "can be more safe or more infallible than the procedure of inductive philosophy as applied to the phenomena of external nature."[19] The tradition of natural theology underpinned the integration of science and religion. Stemming from John Ray and William Derham around the beginning of the eighteenth century, the tradition was most famously championed by William Paley around the beginning of the nineteenth. The natural world, it held, contained evidences of its creator, particularly in the indications of design. Wrote Chalmers:

> When we look on a house with its numerous conveniences, we instantly pronounce it to have been the fruit of contrivance, and that it indicates a contriver; and it is not for a different, but for the very same reason, that when we look on the world with its countless adaptations to the comfort and sustenance of those who live in it, we pronounce it to have been the formation of an architect of adequate skill for devising such a fabric, and adequate powers for carrying his scheme into execution.[20]

Everything has a purpose; therefore, a purposive mind lies behind it; hence, God exists. It seemed a powerful chain of reasoning, and one that could only magnify the wisdom, power, and benevolence of the Almighty as investigation steadily revealed more of his handiwork. Scientific research vindicated Christian theism.

This worldview remained largely convincing, especially to evangelicals, in the mid-nineteenth century. Shortly afterwards, however, it was called into question. In 1859, Charles Darwin published *The Origin of Species* putting forward the idea of evolution. There had been previous proposals of a similar developmental kind. The evolutionary thought of the French naturalist Lamarck had been embraced in radical medical circles, especially

---

[18] T. Chalmers, *A Series of Discourses on the Christian Revelation: Viewed in Connection with the Modern Astronomy*, 4th ed. (Glasgow, 1817), spec. Discourse II.

[19] T. Chalmers, *The Evidence and Authority of the Christian Revelation* (Edinburgh, 1814), p. 191.

[20] T. Chalmers, "Institutes of Theology," in *Posthumous Works of the Reverend Thomas Chalmers*, edited by W. Hanna (Edinburgh, 1849), Vol. I, p. 91.

in London, during the 1830s.[21] In 1844 Robert Chambers of Edinburgh had issued anonymously his *Vestiges of the Natural History of Creation*, arguing that species are uniformly transformed from one to another. Both these innovations, however, were stoutly resisted by evangelicals in the name of the fixity of species. New College, Edinburgh, for example, established a chair of natural science in order to counter theories such as those of Chambers.[22] It was much harder to reject Darwin because of the formidable array of evidence he marshaled in favor of his case. The kernel of the Darwinian challenge to evangelicals was not the questioning of the detail of Genesis: various nonliteral interpretations already existed and so could accommodate the new scientific understanding with relative ease. Rather, the central problem lay in the implications for natural theology. If plants and animals could adapt to the environment of their own accord, the evidence for what Chalmers had called "contrivance" vanished. The Almighty, it seemed, was not the author of the physical features that appeared admirably designed for their purpose. The world no longer furnished proof of the Creator. The traditional defense of the existence of God collapsed, and with it the synthesis of science and religion.

Darwin, however, did not deliver a knockout blow. There was, in fact, less impact on Christian opinion than historians used to suggest. James Moore has shown the most conservative Presbyterians, in particular, were able to absorb the new approach.[23] Many evangelical writers took Darwinism in their stride, simply expanding the scope of natural theology. Free Church thinkers were specially adept at assimilating evolution into a broader vista. John Duns, the occupant of the New College chair of natural science, for

[21] Adrian Desmond, *The Politics of Evolution: Morphology, Medicine and Reform in Radical London* (Chicago, 1989).

[22] Paul Baxter, "Deism and Development: Disruptive Forces in Scottish Natural Theology," in *Scotland in the Age of Disruption*, edited by Stewart J. Brown and Michael Fry (Edinburgh, 1993), pp. 106–108.

[23] J. R. Moore, *The Post-Darwinian Controversies: A Study of the Protestant Struggle to Come to Terms with Darwin in Great Britain and America, 1870–1900* (Cambridge, 1979).

instance, believed that there must be a "frank acceptance of the law of development from lower to higher."[24] He was still able to assert the argument from design, contending now that whole systems rather than individual parts were adapted for their purpose by the Creator's oversight of evolution. Robert Rainy, the colossus bestriding the late nineteenth-century Free Church, had problems with no aspect of Darwinian teaching. In his inaugural address as Principal of New College, Edinburgh, in 1874, he stoutly asserted that no conceivable extension of the idea of evolution could undermine natural theology.[25] Lesser figures lacking Rainy's formidable dialectic skill, however, were often troubled by the challenge to the beliefs they had inherited. John Laidlaw, minister of the Free West Church in Aberdeen, claimed in 1879 that Darwin's principle of natural selection was incredible to believers in an ordered world.[26] Many evangelicals thought it imperative to keep creation distinct from evolution. Many – often the same people – believed it essential to keep humanity outside the evolutionary sequence. And many – perhaps most – wanted to insist that the organic and the inorganic must be kept apart. The distinction between the living and the material must be preserved if there was still to be room for the spiritual and, in the last resort, God. Evolution seemed a threat on all three scores.

By the early 1880s, therefore, Darwin had set a question mark against several aspects of the received Christian worldview. In particular, he had spiked the most powerful gun in the evangelical armory of apologetic, the argument of natural theology from design. Science in the hands of Darwin's militant colleague T. H. Huxley seemed to have turned decisively against religion. Anxieties were abroad in the churches. Drummond refers to his readers being "haunted now by a sense of instability in the foundations of their faith."[27] It was this apprehensive mood that hailed his *Natural*

[24] J. Duns, *Science and Christian Thought* (London, 1866), p. 122.

[25] R. Rainy, *Evolution and Theology: Inaugural Address Delivered in the New College, Edinburgh at the Opening of the Session 1874–75* (Edinburgh, 1874), p. 9.

[26] J. Laidlaw, *The Bible Doctrine of Man* (Edinburgh, 1879), p. 39.

[27] Drummond, *Natural Law*, p. xxiii.

Law in the Spiritual World with relief. Here at last was an author to guide the perplexed in a fresh reconciliation of religion with science. The book achieved success. In the first five years after its publication in 1883, it sold 69,000 copies.[28] By Drummond's death in 1897, there had been twenty-nine editions in Britain alone.[29] By the end of the century, there had been fourteen pirated editions in the United States.[30] Why should Drummond, in particular, have been able to meet the need of the hour?

In the first place, he was not only an evangelical but also an evangelist, a winner of souls. Drummond was not a professional minister. He did preach on a stated basis for a few months during 1876–1877 at Barclay Church, Bruntsfield, in Edinburgh, but he soon abandoned pulpit work and later claimed that he had never delivered regular sermons.[31] He possessed no sense of call to the ministry and did not proceed to ordination immediately after his college course. He was eventually ordained in 1884 only because the step was a condition of assuming a chair of theology in the Free Church College at Glasgow.[32] Again, he later whimsically asserted that he had no recollection of his ordination, and he declared that he would never dare perform a baptism. He refused to use the title "Reverend."[33] Drummond, therefore, possessed a distinctly unclerical image. He was not a traditional minister attached to a settled charge.

Instead, he belonged to the world of the traveling revivalist. In 1873, when he was only 22 and still studying at New College, Edinburgh, the American evangelists Dwight L. Moody and Ira D. Sankey arrived in the city to conduct a campaign. Moody had been a successful shoe salesman in the early years of the mushrooming metropolis of Chicago, a small-scale entrepreneur with a persuasive tongue. He had turned his skills to Y.M.C.A.

[28] Smith, *Drummond*, p. 213.
[29] *The Times*, May 12, 1897, p. 10.
[30] Moore, "Evangelicals and Evolution", p. 386.
[31] J. Y. Simpson, *Henry Drummond* (Edinburgh, 1901), p. 52.
[32] Smith, *Drummond*, p. 246.
[33] John Watson [Ian Maclaren], "Henry Drummond," *North American Review* 164 (May 1897): 521–522.

27

work, selling the Gospel to young men without price. Sankey was at his side to render rather plaintive sacred solos, or lead the audience in more rumbustious choruses, since his calling was "singing the gospel."[34] Here was work for a gifted but unconventional fellow such as Drummond, who threw himself into the Edinburgh campaign. Joining the American pair, he journeyed round the cities of Ireland and England as an additional speaker, especially to young men. He proved a particularly able counselor of prospective converts in the inquiry rooms and was trusted to edit Moody's evangelistic addresses for publication.[35] So passed a whirlwind twenty months. Moody took Britain by storm, nowhere more than in Glasgow, where his visit stimulated the foundation of a battery of causes dedicated to gospel and welfare work. Drummond was wholly identified with Moody's achievement.

After the return of Moody and Sankey to American in 1875, Drummond returned to New College but did not give up mass evangelism. He hired the Gaiety Music Hall in Edinburgh on Sunday evenings, coordinating a series of addresses by his fellow students and sometimes speaking himself.[36] He was to continue similar work in later life. In 1884, the year after the publication of *Natural Law*, there was a visit to Edinburgh by two of the "Cambridge Seven," university men volunteering to carry the gospel to China, giving up prospects of leisured privilege for the sake of arduous missionary adventure. Intense enthusiasm was stirred in the Edinburgh student body, and Drummond was invited to keep the fires of spiritual excitement stoked up.[37] For ten years, on and off, he maintained a series of Sunday evening evangelistic addresses to undergraduates. Success in Edinburgh led to invitations to speak elsewhere: Oxford (1885), German universities (1886), Northfield, Moody's American conference center (1898), and Australia (1890). Drummond became a renowned figure on the international evangelical circuit.

[34] J. F. Findlay, Jr., *Dwight L. Moody: American Evangelist, 1837–1899* (Chicago, 1969).
[35] Simpson, *Drummond*, p. 43.
[36] Smith, *Drummond*, pp. 107–108.
[37] Ibid., pp. 297–298.

A qualification, however, needs to be made about his impact. Moody, it has recently been demonstrated, did sway working-class audiences in Britain and was seen as a herald of popular democracy.[38] Drummond, by contrast, had little appeal for the working people. They did not feel at home with him, according to a contemporary, because, unlike the populist Moody, Drummond seemed too refined.[39] He became a zealous advocate of the Boys' Brigade, founded in Glasgow in 1883 to instill discipline and religion into the urban masses as teenagers, but his contacts were far more with the officers than with the rank and file. The brigade, he once remarked, would have been worth starting "were it only for the sake of the young men who act as officers."[40] It was young men, and especially students, whom Drummond kindled. That meant, in the circumstances of the late nineteenth century, that his message found favor chiefly with an elite group. It was not that he ignored the welfare of the masses. In 1889, he helped plan the Glasgow University Settlement, at which students mingled with the poor to give practical assistance.[41] He even (like many of his contemporaries) modified his theology, giving a larger place to the idea of the kingdom of God, a shorthand for social reconstruction on theological premises.[42] *Natural Law*, furthermore, was originally delivered as separate papers to a working-class audience at the Possil Park mission that Drummond served for four years down to 1882.[43] But the impact of the book was not on the working classes when it appeared in print. It satisfied a more educated reading public.

---

[38] John Coffey, "Democracy and Popular Religion: Moody and Sankey's Mission to Britain, 1873–1875," in *Citizenship and Community: Liberals, Radicals and Collective Identities in the British Isles, 1865–1931*, edited by Eugenio F. Biagini (Cambridge, 1996), pp. 93–119.

[39] Watson, "Drummond," p. 518.

[40] J. Springhall, B. Fraser, and M. Hoare, *Sure and Stedfast: A History of the Boys' Brigade, 1883 to 1983* (London, 1983), pp. 42, 55.

[41] Smith, *Drummond*, p. 286.

[42] H. Drummond, "The Programme of Christianity," in *The Greatest Thing in the World and Other Addresses* (London, 1894).

[43] Smith, *Drummond*, p. 135.

Drummond's message appealed to students because of its simplicity. He denied, for instance, that there was anything mysterious about becoming a Christian. As he put it to Harvard students on another visit to the United States in 1893, "you say, 'I shall follow this teacher and leader until I get a better.' From the time you do that, you are a Christian."[44] The more theologically sophisticated questioned such teaching, but its popularity was undoubted. Yet it was the image, even more than the content, that attracted packed audiences to hear Drummond. Dignified, smartly turned out, with angular features and a drooping moustache, he looked the ideal gentleman.[45] He delivered addresses in beautiful phraseology, and his written style drew the warm commendation of even his sternest critic.[46] Like Gladstone, whom he followed in politics, Drummond possessed a commanding eye. His gaze would penetrate his hearers to the core.[47] Here was a man to respond to, and many did. Drummond's power as a preacher of the gospel, especially among the gilded youth, gave him the highest place in the evangelical pecking order, far above any minister or theologian. His status as an evangelist goes a long way towards explaining the sustained sales of *Natural Law*.

Secondly, however, the welcome given to the book rested on the reputation of Henry Drummond as a scientist. The evangelist's background pointed him towards the sphere of science. He came from a Stirling family of seedsmen, plant breeders as well as suppliers. The members of the firm necessarily took an interest in matters of botanical nurture and classification. Drummond's uncle Peter, usually remembered for launching the Stirling Tract Enterprise, had also shared in founding the Stirling Agricultural Museum, for which, with his half-brother, he had been awarded the gold medal of the Highland and Agricultural Society of

[44] Drummond, *Stones Rolled Away*, p. 37.
[45] Simpson, *Drummond*, pp. 147–148.
[46] J. Denney, On *"Natural Law in the Spiritual World" by a Brother of the Natural Man* (London, 1885), p. 6.
[47] Watson, "Drummond," pp. 515–516.

Scotland.[48] The young Henry spent a number of months assisting his father in the family firm, in the process imbibing some expertise in the science of plants.[49] This experience helps to explain a striking feature of *Natural Law*. The book does not, as one might expect, deal with natural science in general, but, as at least one critic noticed, it concentrates on biological processes alone.[50] The central theme is the "law of biogenesis," that only life gives birth to life. Biology was the scientific domain most familiar to Drummond and, at least in this field, he possessed deeply rooted knowledge.

During his education the evangelist took a variety of scientific courses. At New College, under John Duns, the professor of natural science, Drummond won the first prize in the subject, but in competing with candidates for the ministry, the standard may not have been high. Previously, from 1866 onwards, he had pursued the diverse first-degree curriculum at the University of Edinburgh, passing in mathematics and physics, and in parallel with his mainly theological studies at New College, he took botany, chemistry, zoology, and geology in the university. Although he performed ably in the last two subjects, he twice failed to satisfy the examiners in natural science overall and so left the university without a degree.[51] It may well be that another aspect of his passage through higher education was more formative than the regular curriculum. At that time Drummond took up the characteristic late-Victorian concern with psychic influences. Like Gladstone, he was fascinated by seances; he wrote a paper on "Mesmerism and Animal Magnetism;" and he practiced hypnotism himself.[52] One student was so firmly under his hypnotic powers that when Drummond confronted him on the street, he would meekly surrender his watch at Drummond's suggestion.[53] There is early evidence of an interest

---

[48] M. J. Cormack, *The Stirling Tract Enterprise and the Drummonds* (Stirling, 1984), p. 9.

[49] Simpson, *Drummond*, p. 33.

[50] Denney, *Brother of the Natural Man*, p. 22.

[51] Smith, *Drummond*, pp. 30, 43.

[52] Simpson, *Drummond*, p. 30.

[53] Watson, "Drummond," p. 516.

in the borderlands of the spiritual and the psychological, the religious and the natural. Drummond's *Natural Law in the Spiritual World* was to be founded on the hypothesis that there is a firm connection between the two.

In 1877, after completing his New College training, Drummond was appointed to a lectureship in natural science at its sister Free Church College in Glasgow. There he concentrated not, as might be expected, on apologetics, but on basic science, even performing experiments.[54] He possessed some standing as a practicing scientist, or at least appeared to do so. This feature of his reputation perhaps shows why he exerted a special influence over students of medicine in his weekend addresses at Edinburgh. For many years intending doctors had been notorious for boisterous behavior, but under Drummond's sway, to the delight of the university authorities, they became more restrained.[55] Drummond's professional responsibilities also shed light on the appeal of his book. *Natural Law* was written by a man who earned his bread as a scientist.

What is more, in a typical late-Victorian way, he went off on scientific expeditions. In 1879, with Archibald Geikie, formerly his professor of geology at Edinburgh, he traveled to Canada to examine the strata of the Rocky Mountains, receiving a Fellowship of the Royal Society of Edinburgh in the following year as his reward. In 1883, he was commissioned to survey the natural phenomena, and again especially the geology, of the area between Lakes Nyasa and Tanganyika for the African Lakes Corporation. The result was a vivid account of much of modern Malawi and adjacent parts of Mozambique in *Tropical Africa* (1888). And in 1890, when visiting the New Hebrides at the request of Australian friends in order to observe the political and missionary situation, he also busied himself with scientific observations.[56] Drummond was known as a practitioner of science who enjoyed the confidence of the competent authorities. Although in most disciplines, except geology, he was no more than a gentleman amateur, he could be said to possess a certain reputation in the scientific world.

[54] Simpson, *Drummond*, p. 62.
[55] Watson, "Drummond," p. 522.
[56] Smith, *Drummond*, chapters vii, viii, xv.

Hence, evangelicals felt that they could look to Drummond with confidence on scientific matters. Even though *Natural Law* drew severe criticism from experts, their comments could be regarded as part of the give-and-take of professional debate. Drummond could airily open a public address with a quotation from T. H. Huxley, Darwin's assertively agnostic colleague, as though he was referring to an equal.[57] Huxley is cited seven times in *Natural Law*, and Darwin himself three times.[58] Drummond seemed at home in their company, respecting their views but upholding his own. So his message carried the greater authority. When he insisted in the book that there was a great gulf fixed between the organic and the inorganic, it appeared that a decisive verdict had been passed. Although Huxley entirely shared Drummond's conviction on this point, the most potent threat to Christianity from science seemed to have been abolished by this pronouncement. If there was no continuity between life and the material world, the universe could be fully understood only if there was room for the spiritual. There was still a place for God in his creation. The possibility of a wholly materialistic explanation of the world, long a serious alternative to Christian belief, seemed to be confuted by science itself. Drummond's addition of scientific expertise to evangelistic ardor gave him a unique combination of qualities.

There was, however, a third reason for his celebrity. Drummond was a romantic – not in the sense that he was a quixotic adventurer, though there was an element of that quality in his makeup. Rather he was swayed by the rising intellectual influences of the nine-teenth century, the currents of thought reacting against the Enlightenment of the previous century. Whereas the Enlighten-ment had exalted reason, romanticism appealed to intuition. Starting with the generation of writers of the turn of the century, Wordsworth, Coleridge, Sir Walter Scott, and their circles, a new cultural mood gradually spread to a wider public. By mid-century,

[57] H. Drummond, "The Changed Life," in *The Greatest Thing in the World* (London, 1894), p. 179.
[58] Drummond, *Natural Law*, pp. 23–24, 56, 63, 69n, 287, 289, 290–291; 97, 255, 292.

when Drummond was born, it was supremely embodied in Thomas Carlyle. It favored the dramatic, the historic, the popular, the natural, and the felt. Drummond's educated sensibility could hardly fail to be affected by this spirit of the age.

He duly reveals many leading romantic features in his thought. In *The New Evangelism*, a paper originally read to the Free Church Theological Society in Glasgow, for instance, he asks what is the leading human faculty. It is not, as had been supposed in the past, the faculty of reason; instead it is imagination.[59] The antithesis represents the contrast between the Enlightenment, the Age of Reason, and the romantic, the era of the imagination – and Drummond stands with the romantic. The tone of the new era is pervasive. For the Age of Reason, the dominant metaphor for the understanding of the world was the machine. The universe seemed to operate like a clock, and even human society was treated as an intricate mechanism. For the Romantic Age, however, the dominant metaphor was the tree or the flower. Human beings in particular were pictured as growing like trees, or as gradually coming to flower. Drummond's biological language describes a scene where growth is everywhere. Human beings develop over time, just like plants in the vegetable kingdom. Jesus spoke about the lilies of the field, Drummond declares in a chapter on "Growth" in *Natural Law*, "to teach us how to live a free and natural life, a life which God will unfold for us, without our anxiety, as he unfolds the flower."[60] The prominence of the motif of growth sheds light on an apparently curious point about Drummond. Although he was so close an associate of Moody the revivalist, Drummond is said not to have fully understood sudden conversion.[61] In *Natural Law*, he endorses the principle that people do become Christians instantaneously, but remarks that probably for the majority the moment is unconscious. Then, having insisted that new life normally originates at a specific juncture, he immediately stresses that "Growth is the work of time."[62] Development, not crisis, is

[59] Drummond, *New Evangelism*, pp. 26, 28.
[60] Drummond, *Natural Law*, p. 123.
[61] Simpson, *Drummond*, p. 43.
[62] Drummond, *Natural Law*, pp. 93–94.

his major theme, for human beings are like seedlings that eventually blossom into flower. "Salvation," as he puts it, "is a definite process."[63] Drummond was working from romantic premises. That is because of the intellectual influences that played on him.

It is true that the strongest individual factor in the genesis of *Natural Law* was Herbert Spencer, who provided the evolutionary framework of thought and who is cited far more than any other author.[64] Spencer, though stressing development, is not usually classified as a romantic. Other writers who molded Drummond's thinking, however, belong in a strong sense to the romantic school. His eye for nature was sharpened by John Ruskin, the art critic celebrated as one of the greatest romantic prose writers.[65] He quotes Ruskin in *Natural Law*[66] and again at the opening of the preface to his later book, *The Ascent of Man*.[67] Drummond's mind was stimulated by the American Transcendentalists, the group that marked the first reception of romantic thought into the United States. Drummond found R. W. Emerson soothing and warmed to his optimism; W. E. Channing taught him reverence for God as a moral being. A favorite theological writer was F. F. W. Robertson of Brighton, the Carlyle of the Church of England.[68] And Thomas Carlyle himself is praised in *Natural Law* for his "eloquent preaching of the Gospel of Work."[69] These writers shaped Drummond's mind, giving it the characteristic romantic turn.

The symptoms of the romantic approach are evident in the substance of Drummond's teaching. One is the prioritizing of feeling over reason, the supposition that experience cannot be captured in words. It leads to a distinctly antidoctrinal position. In *Natural Law*, Drummond remarks at one point that the worst enemy of a living church is "propositional theology."[70] He constantly downgrades doctrine in the scheme of things. The New

---

[63] Drummond, *Natural Law*, p. 109.
[64] Moore, "Evangelicals and Evolution."
[65] Simpson, *Drummond*, p. 31.
[66] Drummond, *Natural Law*, p. 173.
[67] H. Drummond, *The Ascent of Man* (London, 1894), p. v.
[68] Simpson, *Drummond*, p. 32.
[69] Drummond, *Natural Law*, p. 349. Carlyle is also cited at pp. 7–8, 316, 341.
[70] Ibid., p. 360.

Evangelism, he says, must not be doctrinal.[71] Religion, he claims, is not a matter of thinking but of living.[72] In part this aspect of his message is of a piece with his unclerical stance: there is no need for the technicalities of professional theological terminology. At a deeper level, however, it is typical of the late nineteenth-century eagerness to repudiate sharply defined doctrine. The tendency was clearest among Unitarians and Broad Church Anglicans, but it was also evident among broader evangelicals. Religion, for these people, was a thing of beauty that could be damaged by any reduction to hard logical sentences. Drummond expresses this mood to the full in the pages of *Natural Law*. He deplores attempts to set out "cut and dry" theology and actually praises "vagueness" as a sign of truth. "You cannot live on theological forms," he contends, "without . . . ceasing to be a man."[73] This aversion to doctrine locates Drummond within a romantically inspired trend of the times.

Insofar as he did express doctrinal views, he seemed suspiciously broad – especially to the Highland presbyteries of his church that censured him for heretical tendencies.[74] Drummond, for example, dismissed the federal theology of seventeenth-century Calvinism as "an elaborate rationalism."[75] In keeping with his reaction against the Enlightenment, reason must not rule. Hence, his message could be remarkably liberal for its day. Unlike most evangelists, for instance, he rarely spoke of the need for repentance.[76] The weakness of his teaching on sin, in fact, induced certain other evangelists to refuse to appear on the same platform with him. The orthodox at Moody's Northfield Conference in 1893, Drummond reported, "fell upon me and rent me."[77] And there were other indications of an advanced theological position. In *Natural Law*, Drummond cites the American liberal Congregationalist Horace Bushnell and

---

[71] Drummond, *New Evangelism*, p. 20.
[72] Drummond, *Stones Rolled Away*, p. 33.
[73] Drummond, *Natural Law*, pp. 360, 363.
[74] Simpson, *Drummond*, p. 96.
[75] Drummond, *New Evangelism*, p. 27.
[76] Watson, "Drummond," p. 523.
[77] Smith, *Drummond*, p. 421.

the English Unitarian James Martineau with equal approval.[78] Likewise, Drummond treated J. R. Seeley's *Ecce Homo*, which had alienated evangelicals on its appearance in 1865 for describing Jesus in solely human terms, as an invaluable work: he called it his "stand-by." Drummond was even willing to repudiate an article of the creed, for he rejected the doctrine of the resurrection of the body as too materialistic.[79] The spiritual must take precedence over the physical. The liberal tendency should be seen as another effect of his romantic approach to the Christian faith.

If this cast of mind explains why theological conservatives were wary of Drummond, it also helps to show why *Natural Law* made so profound an impression. The old harmonization of science and religion through a natural theology grounded on Enlightenment premises had, as we have seen, been undermined. Drummond presented an alternative version of natural theology based on fresh romantic presuppositions. The inherited static, mechanistic categories were replaced by dynamic, organic views. The Free Church theologian James Denney, who clung to an Enlightenment worldview predicated on hard facts, found *Natural Law* an entirely unconvincing work. It was, he concluded, "a book that no lover of men will call religious, and no student of theology scientific."[80] Drummond's writings were entirely alien to Denney. To an evangelical public that had read Scott and Carlyle, Wordsworth and Ruskin, however, *Natural Law* came as a breath of fresh air. Here, notwithstanding the doctrinal imprecision, was a vision of the universe as process. Evolution was its method, but God was in charge. Drummond's book offered a new type of natural theology, bringing together science and religion on fresh intellectual premises. His synthesis suited a climate of opinion suffused by romanticism.

Of Drummond's other writings, *The Ascent of Man* (1894), the evangelist's Lowell Lectures, was less successful than *Natural Law*. It contended that the selfish struggle for life revealed by Darwin was accompanied by something altruistic, the struggle for the life of others, in both nature and humanity. In the end,

---

[78] Drummond, *Natural Law*, pp. 140, 168.
[79] Simpson, *Drummond*, pp. 154, 155.
[80] Denney, *Brother of the Natural Man*, p. 67.

Christianity and evolution were one because both produced love.[81] As Drummond's obituarist in *The Times* admitted, the book was severely criticized by scientists and theologians alike.[82] It was not a foundation of his fame either in his own day or subsequently. It has been suggested that another legacy was more important than either *The Ascent of Man* or *Natural Law*. Drummond's lecture on the paean to love in I Corinthians 13, *The Greatest Thing in the World* (1890), sold even more widely than *Natural Law* and is still in print today.[83] The booklet has been an enduring source of Christian devotional inspiration. Nevertheless, it has much less significance for wider developments in the world of thought. *Natural Law*, by contrast, stands as a landmark in the relations of religion and science.

What, then, accounts for its popularity? Henry Drummond wrote at a time when traditional natural theology had been fundamentally challenged by Darwin. The argument from design that was so convincing to minds steeped in Enlightenment assumptions had been evacuated of persuasive power. Christians found that science now posed a formidable threat to religion. To many in the international evangelical movement, Drummond seemed to provide an answer. He was an evangelist, and therefore, trustworthy; he was a scientist, and therefore, authoritative; he was a romantic, and therefore, supplied a new integration of science and religion suited to the taste of the times. In the end, he may have failed to convince his more discerning readers. Others, such as the Anglo-Catholic theologian Aubrey Moore, may have slotted evolution into a Christian worldview far more satisfactorily.[84] Yet, at a particular juncture, Drummond was the man of the hour. Evangelistic work, the practice of science and romanticism: in the late-Victorian years these three seemed to constitute a triple cord that could not easily be broken.

[81] Drummond, *The Ascent of Man*, p. 438.
[82] *The Times*, March 12, 1897, p. 10.
[83] J. M. Wysong, "Henry Drummond," in *Dictionary of Scottish Church History and Theology*, edited by N. M. de S. Cameron (Edinburgh, 1993), p. 258.
[84] A. L. Moore, *Science and the Faith* (London, 1889).

3

ᏝᏝᏝ

Henry Drummond (1851–1897): a postscript

Robin S. Barbour

The reason why I have been asked to say something this afternoon is a purely personal one. Although I quite plainly never knew Henry Drummond, since we are celebrating the centenary of his death, I knew of him from very early days. A large marble plaque, with his head and shoulders in bas-relief, hung on the staircase wall in the house where I was brought up. My father explained to me at an early age that this was someone who had been my grandfather's very greatest friend. My grandfather Robert Barbour, after whom I was called, had died when he was only 37, and he too, like Drummond, was a hero of my early days. Quite why these two great friends were such marvelous men I think I took some time to discover; but it was plain that one thing they shared was a very lively sense of humour, and another was a tremendous devotion to the Christian faith and its proclamation.

They became friends when both were at the University of Edinburgh, and their friendship was cemented at New College, the Free Church's theological college in Edinburgh, after my great-grandmother had persuaded Henry Drummond not to yield to the attempts of D. L. Moody and Ira D. Sankey, the American evangelists, to go off to the U.S.A. in their wake while he was still a student, but to return to college to complete his degree. Already at the age of 23, Drummond had had enormous success as an evangelist working with Moody and Sankey in this country, and his devotion to this work, especially as it related to students, never left him; but he was also, he tells us, very grateful to old Mrs. Barbour for her stern advice, administered while he was suffering from a sprained ankle and couldn't get away.

The picture of Drummond which I got from my father and from others was of the most rounded character – I think that is the way to put it – they had ever known, a man of enormous capacity in a large number of directions. His college friends called him "the prince." Of his intellectual ability there can be no doubt, but he also retained a boyishness, a love of fun, of cricket and football, and indeed, a love of boys, throughout the 45 years of his life. He was a lover of the open air and a skilled fly fisherman; Loch Stack in Sutherland was said to be his favourite. He was perhaps as good an example as one could find of the educated, aspiring, middle class, talented and principled Scots who contributed so enormously to the life and welfare both of Britain and of many other lands during the Victorian era. But if he was a man of aspirations, they were of no selfish or this-worldly kind: it was the spread of Christ's Gospel, and that alone, that lay at the centre of his aspirations – even of his scientific work. For he was convinced – and this as much as anything is what made him a figure of real importance in his day – that the scientific achievement and the advance of faith had but one aim and purpose in the end, namely the glory of God.

There is one other thing that I think I should say about him at this stage. He was, quite plainly, one of the most effective speakers it would be possible to imagine, in a day when the unaided spoken word was of far greater influence than it is today. But his appeal seems never to have been in the first instance to the emotions, contrast most evangelists today. He sought to convince, to speak to the human reason, and then to convict. He had a brilliant command of language and style; to this day one is arrested by his vivid, terse, eloquent, and utterly economical way of speaking and writing. He had a great sympathy with those who were impatient with the church, as he himself no doubt often was, and this no doubt endeared him to many and helped them on their road to faith.

It must also be said that he must have been a truly exceptional pastor, with an early acquired insight into the twists and turns of the human conscience. He spent untold hours wrestling with people who needed his help and got it unstintingly, and he could speak easily and naturally with and to people of all walks in society. His London lectures in Grosvenor House, organized initially by Lord and Lady Aberdeen, were quite plainly not tailored expressly to his distinguished audience, but equally plainly they hit their target well.

But if Henry Drummond was a remarkable evangelist, it was as a scientific thinker and a bringer together of the apparently contradictory understandings of the world represented by science and religion that he was best known. Professor Cheyne and Dr. Bebbington have spoken about this, and I think that perhaps I should just add three points if I may.

The first is that it seems to me impossible to exaggerate the importance in the world of the decades after Darwin's *Origin of Species* of any sincere attempt to bring together the worlds of science and religion, and make of those two apparently contradictory universes of discourse a single whole. After all, the world is one, and must in the end be understood as such. In this context, Drummond's assertion in his first great book *Natural Law in the Spiritual World* that the laws of the natural world and the laws of the spiritual world were not merely similar but actually identical, must have seemed breathtaking in its originality and its interpretative power. This is not the place to argue the case – and we must never forget that Drummond's work immediately met with very powerful criticisms as well as with an enormous and enthusiastic readership – but perhaps, I might make just one point in this area, really as an illustration of something more general about Drummond and his significance.

Rereading parts of *Natural Law in the Spiritual World*, I have been impressed by the way in which Drummond there allowed his tremendous conviction about the importance of the principle of biogenesis, and its applicability right across the natural world, to drive him into a strange theological position, which perhaps unconsciously he owed in some ways to his traditional Calvinist

41

background, and that is this: the whole of human civic and moral life is assigned to the world of nature and natural law, and the spiritual world, or the world of grace, is kept very firmly removed from it. This may remind us, not only of Calvin but also of the early Barth, but it was not, I think, really characteristic of Drummond's deepest convictions; and the point I want to make is that Drummond was not a systematic theologian. The systems of his thought had practical aims, and whether they were scientific in nature or theological – and the two were never far apart in his mind – they might well be abandoned as the world moved on, and his thought moved on, and the needs of the current situation moved on, too. So it was that when he came to write his later Lowell Lectures on *The Ascent of Man,* his thought on the matter of the natural world and the world of grace had moved on. His starting point now was that world of grace, the spiritual world and its laws, and so he came to a much wider understanding of the operation of the Holy Spirit in the world. He was writing of course under the very strong influence of Darwin and all he stood for; and yet his views in the end seem to come closer to those of Lamarck, than to those of Darwin. He was an optimist, because also a theist and a Christian, and Darwin's deep pessimism was alien to him.

The second thing that I would like to mention concerns Drummond's great emphasis on altruism within the evolutionary process. This will awaken some echoes within the current scene. The late Professor Vero Wynne-Edwards of Aberdeen, whom I was fortunate to know as a colleague, did some pioneering work on that theme, and it deserves to be carefully considered still. It is, of course, totally at variance with the understanding of Professor Richard Dawkins with his "selfish gene." I am not competent to add more here, but I think that the issue remains an important one.

Finally, I would like to stress that Drummond's so-called "modernism" always had evangelistic as well as apologetic motives. If he departed from traditional understandings, it was never, I think, simply because he wanted to keep within the "spirit of the age" but always also because he saw the new view he espoused as the necessary understanding of the Gospel's offer and demand (always both of those things, offer and demand; never just one). Perhaps, I might illustrate this by quoting from one of his so-called Christmas booklets, where he is speaking about the "Day of Vengeance." He writes:

> When is that day? It is now. Who is the Avenger? Law. [Can't elaborate on this now, but it is interesting]. What law? Criminal law. Sanitary Law. Social Law. Natural Law. . . . Wherever the poor are trodden upon or tread upon one another; wherever the air is poison and the water foul; wherever want stares and vice reigns and rags rot – there the Avenger takes his stand. . . . Delay him not. He is the messenger of Christ. His Day dawns slowly, but his work is sure. Though evil stalks the world, it is on the way to execution; though wrong reigns, it must end in self-combustion. The very nature of things is God's Avenger; the very story of civilisation is the history of Christ's throne.

So Drummond wrote, and links could be made with many a writer since then, Reinhold Niebuhr for example, and the liberation theologians, too. Drummond is still important, not only because he sought a synthesis between religious and scientific under-standings of the world, a synthesis which was for a short time immensely influential, but was perhaps never really viable – in that respect he recalls Teilhard de Chardin – but also because he threw out ideas at many points and in many ways which other thinkers, more systematic than he, took up and developed. It is indeed right that he should be commemorated in the land of his birth, and I do commend the initiative and the organizing ability of that contemporary terrorist (where is he?) Eric Motley whose work has made this gathering possible.

4

❧

"Apples of gold in pictures of silver": Henry Drummond and "words fitly spoken"

Thomas E. and Marla Haas Corts

Even with the perspective of a hundred years, Henry Drummond does not fit easily into the one-word descriptions we tend to require of the well-known. He was a scientist of sorts, a philosopher–theologian, a lecturer, an ordained minister, a professor, an evangelist, a traveler, an author. His mind worked in a logical manner, and his quest for a reasonable faith led him to seek reconciliation between traditional Christian views and the emerging science of his day. But more than any single role, Henry Drummond was a professional man of words. He made his living and his life as a listener and thinker, and as a practitioner of the art of discourse.

Words have been silent custodians of the ideas and good name of Henry Drummond since his voice was stilled by an untimely death in 1897. In both spoken and written form, he respected the power of language and employed it in a clear, unaffected and persuasive manner, as though persuaded by the writer of Proverbs that "a word fitly spoken is like apples of gold in pictures of silver" (Proverbs 25:11, King James). How did the reflective young man – wrapping his expression in a lucid *gravitas*, saturated with sincerity, projected in a calm, modest voice, emphasized by a

45

penetrating gaze and a caring countenance – how did he come to spellbind large audiences at age 22 and publish a best-seller at 32? Why is he one of the select English-language authors still in print and never out-of-print more than one hundred years after his death? What made Henry Drummond such a powerful *persona*?

A contemporary publication offered one simple view: "Young men thronged to hear him because his manly nature appealed to their manliness, and because he solved their doubts without asking them to deny their reason."[1] From his earliest work with Moody, Drummond's friend, W. Robertson Nicoll, wrote: "He made himself a great speaker; he knew how to seize the critical moment, and his modesty, his refinement, his gentle and generous nature, his manliness, and, above all, his profound conviction, won for him disciples in every place he visited."[2] "An [unidentified] Edinburgh gentleman," and close friend said, "Professor Drummond was a charming personality. No one could associate with him without feeling the attraction of his manner, and no public gathering which he addressed could resist what, for want of a better phrase, must be called his magnetic influence."[3] This effect Drummond had on listeners was both immediate and long term. As Nicoll wrote, "No wonder that his speech often produced a magical instantaneous effect. But he left seeds in many minds which fructified in a way of which the world knew nothing."[4]

By any standard, Henry Drummond was an effective communicator. Widely known in Scotland for his work with evangelist Dwight L. Moody even before his twenty-third birthday, world fame enveloped the young author with publication of his *Natural Law in the Spiritual World* in 1883. Nicoll, who despite their friendship could be critical of Drummond, stated that "Whatever

[1] "The Outlook" quoted in *The Chautauquan* (May 1897), p. 203.

[2] W. Robertson Nicoll, "A Memorial Sketch" in *The Ideal Life and Other Unpublished Addresses*, by Henry Drummond (London, 1897), pp. 8–9.

[3] *The Glasgow Herald*, March 12, 1897.

[4] W. Robertson Nicoll, "Professor Henry Drummond," *The British Weekly* 21 (March 18, 1897), p. 1.

criticisms may be passed, it will be allowed that few men in the century have done so much to bring their hearers and readers to the feet of Jesus Christ."[5] Nicoll "doubted whether any living novelist has had so many readers, and perhaps no living writer has been so eagerly followed and so keenly discussed on the Continent and in America."[6] He claimed for Drummond "the widest vogue" from Norway to Germany, and believed that scarcely a week passed in Germany without publication of a book or pamphlet in which his views were canvassed.[7]

The classical modes used by speakers included *ethos, pathos, logos*. Clearly, Drummond employed all three, but used *pathos* least. Indeed, he seemed at times almost afraid of emotion. When, on his first visit to America, he visited one of Moody's meetings, he was surprised and pleased to find that the service was calm and not emotion-charged.[8] He noted that he did not want cleverness or ostentation in speech among those who were part of the deputation teams sent out in behalf of the Edinburgh student work.[9] While he seemed clearly to prefer a rational approach to belief, his own high character was a profound factor in his perceived credibility, as though in fulfillment of Quintilian's dictum that the perfect orator is "a good man speaking well."[10]

His credibility was high. In Simpson's estimate, "Herein lay a great part of the secret of his power. Men felt that what he said was true to the man who uttered the words; he produced in his hearers and readers the conviction that he told them of

[5] Nicoll, "Memorial Sketch," p. 17. In a letter to Dr. Marcus Dods, minister friend of Nicoll and Drummond, Christmas Eve, 1898, Nicoll wrote regarding George Adam Smith's biography of Drummond: ". . . The book confirms what I never could help feeling – that Drummond was a charlatan, in the sense that he was always trying tasks far beyond him. . . ." See T. H. Darlow, *William Robertson Nicoll: Life and Letters* (London, 1925), p. 163.

[6] Nicoll, "Memorial Sketch," p. 1.

[7] Ibid., p. 1.

[8] George Adam Smith, *The Life of Henry Drummond*, 2nd ed. (London, 1899), p. 139.

[9] T. J. Shanks, ed., *A College of Colleges: Led By D. L. Moody* (Chicago, 1887), pp. 249–251.

[10] Quintilian, XII.ii.1.

things through which he himself had lived, and so had found to be real."[11]

A medical student who attended his meetings while at Edinburgh later recalled that Drummond's immense influence was due to solid reasons, but mostly due to "his own personality and pure spirit."[12] The writer John Watson, friend of Drummond from boyhood, echoed that judgment, saying, "His influence, more than that of any man I have ever met, was mesmeric – which means that while other men affect their fellows by speech and example, he seized one directly by his living personality."[13]

Much of his influence appears to have emanated from solid character. D. L. Moody knew most of the spiritual giants of his time, the great preachers of England and America, evangelicals and leaders of the Keswick conference. To a mutual friend, Moody said that Drummond was "the sweetest tempered Christian" he ever knew.[14] At Drummond's death, Moody wrote: "No man has ever been with me for any length of time, but I could see some things in him that were unlike Christ, and I often see them in myself; but I never saw them in Henry Drummond. He is the most Christlike man I ever knew."[15]

And Drummond's close friend, John Watson, himself famous under the pen-name Ian Maclaren, wrote:

> One takes for granted that each man has his besetting sin, and we could name that of our friends, but Drummond was an exception to this rule. After a lifetime's intimacy I do not remember my friend's failing. . . . Henry Drummond was the most perfect Christian I have ever known or expect to see this side the grave.[16]

---

[11] James Y. Simpson, *Henry Drummond*, Famous Scots Series (Edinburgh, 1901), p. 154.

[12] George Newman, quoted in Smith, *Drummond*, p. 331.

[13] John Watson, "A Memorial Sketch" in *The Ideal Life and Other Unpublished Addresses*, by Henry Drummond (London, 1897), p. 27.

[14] William R. Moody, *The Life of Dwight L. Moody* (New York, 1900), p. 310.

[15] Moody to James Stalker, quoted in Smith, *Drummond*, p. 9.

[16] John Watson [Ian Maclaren], "Henry Drummond," *North American Review* 164 (May 1897): 525.

Such paeans of praise were earned within an abbreviated life span. By the time of his death at age 45, he had extensive travels and successful publications to his credit, but he was still quite young when his uncommon ability first gained notice. His earliest speaking before others must have occurred during student days at the University of Edinburgh, when he debated and made presentations to a student society and later to the Theological Society. But he did not consider such opportunities before classmates as "public," for in a diary he referenced what he regarded as his "first public appearance." In the fall of 1873, asked to give the closing prayer at a congregational prayer meeting at the Riego Street Mission of St. Cuthbert's Free Church, the 22-year-old recorded his response.

> The first time I ever faced an audience, sensations not remarkable. When my turn came I trembled on standing up – considerably all through. Tremor in voice. I should not think perceived; mind kept perfectly clear and cool. Voice seemed not my own, but a new voice. Have no possible idea how it sounded. Prayer was simple and to the point. It was outlined in thought during the afternoon – a sentence or two were written, but then not all remembered at the time.[17]

Cautiously, he had followed a conclusion reached a few years earlier: he was more effective speaking extemporaneously than when writing out statements beforehand.[18]

Less than a year after describing his earliest attempt at public prayer, this same youth was fearlessly facing thousands who found him a compelling speaker. The opportunity was provided by Moody and Sankey, whose ministry in Scotland evoked greater response than in England. Needing help in continuing meetings and in following up their events, they turned to young ministerial students at New College, Edinburgh – among them Drummond and friends James Stalker and John Ewing. It was an unprecedented experience for young ministers-to-be, first in the "inquiry room," a sort of laboratory of human concerns peopled by seekers responding to

[17] Smith, *Drummond*, p. 52.
[18] Ibid., p. 53.

Moody's message and invitation. A short time later they gave brief testimonies, and finally they had major responsibility for planning and executing special services, including full-length sermons, following in the wake of the American evangelists. Stalker has described the students' first appearance at such a meeting in Glasgow's Ewing Place Congregational Church. After a powerful sermon by a local minister, the students spoke briefly, one after the other. Moody closed the service with a request for those desiring prayer to fill the front rows. Unlike anything Glasgow had seen previously, 101 persons responded to Moody's plea, and for years afterward it was referred to as "One-hundred-one Night."[19] Stalker noted that the six young testifiers had carefully observed the entire event, went back to their hotel that night, and stayed up late reviewing the experience. Such occasions were remarkable opportunities for young men intent on ministry.

The speaker's concern for his audience: mass meetings versus personal encounters

Even with this early exposure to, and his later success with, mass meetings, most of his life, Drummond seems to have been ambivalent about the effectiveness of mass gatherings, versus one-to-one conversations. In one of his essays written as a divinity student, he contrasted the modern desire for mass meetings with the manner in which Jesus had dealt with persons – in twos and threes, and ones. He explained:

> The past has indeed no masses. *Men*, not masses, have done all that is great in history, in science, and in religion. . . . But the capacity of acting upon individuals is now almost a lost art. . . . Christianity began with one. We have forgotten the simple way of the Founder of the greatest influence the world has ever seen – how He ran away from cities, how He shirked the crowds, how He lagged behind the rest at Samaria to have a quiet talk with *one* humble Syro-Phoenician woman.[20]

[19] Smith, *Drummond*, pp. 64–65.
[20] Henry Drummond, "Spiritual Diagnosis," in *The New Evangelism and Other Papers*, 2nd ed. (London, 1899), pp. 192–193.

But as early as 1870, in his university valedictory address as president of the Philomathic Society, Drummond had stated: "The lecture is the best means. If it has failed into disrepute in our day, that is because there are no good lecturers."[21]

Later, when he advised how to conduct a young men's meeting, he seemed down on the lecture method and strong on brevity, suggesting two short talks of about ten minutes each as more suitable for young men than a long sermon. He wrote: "The addresses may be anything but preaching – young men will not stand being preached at by one another. Individual testimonies to personal change of heart have been found most useful of all."[22]

But after working in Moody's inquiry room, he learned something about more personal intimacy, of face-to-face, heart-to-heart communication in which empathy and sympathy create a rapport, when confidences are shared and candor prevails – conditions impossible by the very nature of mass meetings and the quantity of souls present. In an 1882 letter to his friend Robert Barbour, Drummond wrote: "I must say I believe in personal dealing more and more every day and in the inadequacy of mere preaching."[23]

And years later, contemplating the Grosvenor House meetings, he wrote his friend Lord Aberdeen: "I must not disguise from you also that I would have little faith in my lecturing producing any permanent result. The lecture, as a weapon, always has seemed to me a poor influence in religion. . . . I should really have some faith in addresses of a simple kind – not written lectures, but clear statements of what Christianity really is, what personal religion really is. . . ."[24]

Perhaps it was his enormous capacity for compassion and friendship that made him so effective in the inquiry room. Stalker wrote that "often he was to be seen going home through the streets after a meeting with a man in whose arm his own was

[21] Smith, *Drummond*, p. 3.

[22] Cuthbert Lennox [J. H. Napier], *Henry Drummond: A Biographical Sketch*, 4th ed. (London, 1902), p. 40.

[23] Letter, Drummond to Barbour, March 13, 1882, quoted in Smith, *Drummond*, p. 134.

[24] Smith, *Drummond*, p. 254.

linked."[25] Oft-quoted was his statement that he heard such "tales of woe" in Moody's inquiry room that at times he felt he needed to change his clothes after the contact.[26] His biographer related the story told by the lady of a home in which Drummond stayed. She said the household was having evening prayers when Drummond came in and, leaving the others, she went down to see if the ox-tail soup was hot and ready for him. She found Drummond leaning with his head bowed on the mantel, his gaze penetrating the fire. When she spoke to him, he peered up, looking haggard and worn, and she asked if he were tired. He answered, "No, not very. But oh, I am sick with the sins of these men! How can God bear it?"[27]

His profound interest in all persons was well-known, spanning all levels of a class-conscious society from nobility to common folks, the eccentric and special, to university students and children. In the parlance of the day, John Watson wrote: ". . . he had many friends. Some of them were street arabs, some were negroes, some were medicals, some were evangelists, some were scientists, some were theologians, some were nobles."[28] The week following his death, *The British Weekly* stated: ". . . no man was more familiar with the battles and defeats of his fellows. . . . The incalculable work he did as a father confessor of multitudes was apparently accomplished with triumphant ease. He was always willing to hear, to help, and to give, but he himself never asked anything, never seemed to need anything. . . ."[29] Smith concluded, ". . . his sympathy continued to be about him, as it were, the walls of a quiet and healing confessional, into which wounded men and women crept from the world, dared 'to unlock the heart and let it speak' – dared to tell him the worst about themselves. It is safe to say that no man in our generation can have heard confession more constantly than Drummond did."[30] The same thought

[25] Ibid., p. 64.
[26] Ibid., p. 100.
[27] Ibid., p. 333.
[28] Watson, "Memorial Sketch," p. 23.
[29] *The British Weekly*, March 18, 1897.
[30] Smith, *Drummond*, p. 11.

is echoed in Nicoll's statement, "He received, I venture to say, more of the confidences of people untouched by the ordinary work of the Church than any other man of his time."[31] And Simpson, whose entire family had been close to Drummond, wrote that "Drummond's peculiar power resulted in his being constituted the confessor and confidant of vast numbers of his fellow-creatures. Possibly no man of his generation had such an intense acquaintance with humanity, both on the vertical and horizontal planes, and yet he did not become a cynic."[32]

Drummond's concern for common folks was a lifelong hallmark. He was at ease with the working class people of Possil Park Church, where he ministered effectively for four years, and with whom he had shared the substance of what became *Natural Law in the Spiritual World*. He helped the Aberdeens form the Associated Workers League in London and encouraged them with their innovative Haddo House Association, which afforded recognition, training, and instruction to domestic workers and field hands.[33] He inspired student voluntarism with the Glasgow University Settlement, and helped open a new work, the "Pleasant Sunday Afternoon" for the men of the Port Dundas district of Glasgow.[34] He said, "My conviction, indeed, grows stronger every day that the masses require and deserve the very best work we have. The crime of evangelism is laziness; and the failure of the average mission church to reach intelligent working men rises from the indolent reiteration of threadbare formulae by teachers, often competent enough, who have not first learned to respect their hearers."[35]

Not only common folks, but children had a special bond with Drummond. His work with the Boys' Brigade movement was second only to his work with university students. Smith wrote of a special backpack Drummond had constructed to reduce the strain of heavy loads Glasgow child-workers were compelled to carry

[31] Nicoll, "Memorial Sketch," p. 2.

[32] Simpson, *Drummond*, pp. 148–149.

[33] Smith, *Drummond*, p. 281; Lord and Lady Aberdeen, *We Twa: Reminiscences of Lord and Lady Aberdeen*, 2 vols. (London, 1925), Vol. I, pp. 195–196.

[34] Smith, *Drummond*, p. 462.

[35] Ibid., p. 147.

down city streets.[36] Drummond was responsible for starting the Boys' Brigade in Australia, and he promoted it vigorously in America and Canada.[37] The children of friends became very special to him. In her biography of her husband, Mrs. George Adam Smith recalled of Drummond that ". . . he was like a young uncle to our children. He used often to come to our home to play with them in the hour before their bedtime, and he took our little boys to their first circus."[38] Lennox wrote, "If Drummond was in the house, children were wont to consider no one else of equal importance. He had a rich repertoire of conundrums and stories of adventure; there were few indoor or outdoor games with which he was not familiar. . . ."[39] He came to write children's stories and to assist Lady Aberdeen and her daughter with their children's magazine, *Wee Willie Winkie*, editing it for a time (1891–1892) – something hardly expected of the average professor with a world-wide reputation.[40] Lady Aberdeen wrote in her memoirs that Drummond was "the playmate and boon companion of our children. . . ."[41]

In addition to common folks and children, Drummond made room for the odd and unusual among humankind. Stalker wrote:

> His patience with bores was his friends' wonder to the end; but he dearly liked to come across the unconventional, the Bohemian, and the vagrant. Showmen of all sorts were such joy to him, and he got on so well with them, that we used to nickname him Barnum. A Spanish guitar-player, a laddie who performed on the penny whistle, music-hall singers, a cornet-player, a concertina-player – he had a knack of picking them out.[42]

He reserved a special fondness for Moolu, his African retainer on his expedition to that continent in 1883–1884, and praised Moolu

[36] Ibid., p. 445.

[37] Ibid., p. 450.

[38] Lilian Adam Smith, *George Adam Smith: A Personal Memoir and Family Chronicle* (London, 1944), p. 78.

[39] Lennox, *Drummond*, p. 180.

[40] Ibid., p. 183.

[41] Lord and Lady Aberdeen, *We Twa*, p. 204.

[42] Quoted in Smith, *Drummond*, pp. 98–99.

that "he did his duty and never told a lie."[43] On his trip to America, one of the memories of his mentor, Sir Archibald Geikie, was "How he [Drummond] would draw out our attendants over the camp-fire at night, getting each to cap the other's thrilling and incredible tales of adventure!"[44] In America, he once volunteered to assist with a curious funeral among ragtag gold-miners in the frontier area of Boulder, Colorado. He found the miners fascinating and wrote that "the diggers were a very rough lot – kindly, brave, but wild and lawless."[45]

Clearly, "all kinds of men interested Drummond, but none more so than those who were in some way handicapped or had broken down. In his own house, it was almost pitiful to see how anyone with a genuine tale of distress could steal his late evening work hours, as he stood in the vestibule leaning against a mantelshelf, patiently listening."[46]

So good was Drummond, one-on one, that Stalker wrote: "He worked hard in the inquiry rooms; but shy men who would not stand up in a meeting, nor enter an inquiry room, waited for him by the doors as he came out, or waylaid him in the street, or wrote asking him for an interview. He took great trouble with every one of them, as much trouble and interest as if each was a large meeting."[47] And by Stalker's analysis: "He was not at his best in addressing very large meetings; but in an audience not exceeding five hundred his quiet voice and simple manner found their range."[48]

He had an uncommon capacity to ". . . put himself alongside the most hopeless, the most desperate of human souls. . . . Strange individuals of every calling, honorable and the reverse, felt that they could trust him, nor was their trust misplaced."[49]

---

[43] Watson, *Drummond*, p. 516.

[44] Smith, *Drummond*, p. 188.

[45] Letter, Drummond to his mother, August 21, 1879. Unless otherwise noted, all letters referenced are from the Drummond Papers in the National Library of Scotland.

[46] Simpson, *Drummond*, p. 15.

[47] Stalker, quoted in Smith, *Drummond*, p. 98.

[48] Ibid., p. 97.

[49] Simpson, *Drummond*, p. 44.

Teaching also afforded Drummond a close connection to individuals. In his era, Free Church College at Glasgow enrolled between seventy and one hundred. Drummond's responsibility was to a first-year class of twelve to twenty-four, and he chose to lecture them on the rudiments of geology, botany, and general methods of modern science. His custom was to end the year with several days' "geologising in Arran," a rugged island popular with hikers, off the west coast of Scotland.[50]

His ideas

The grist for Henry Drummond's discourses was refined from traditional Christian beliefs. He enjoyed taking a commonly quoted scripture and developing a new and different application. Freshness was a much-prized fruit of Drummond's thinking. "His purpose was not just to restate the old truths in new language but to provide a new basis for corroborating the old truths, new proof which would stand under the scrutiny of a scientific age."[51] "Perhaps his main characteristic both as speaker and writer was his brilliant and untiring freshness. You might agree with him, or you might not, but you could not choose but hear and remember."[52] With training in science, he had sharpened his powers of observation. His study of divinity had helped him raise important questions. During his theological studies, a summer at Tübingen, then an incubator of biblical higher criticism, may have conditioned him toward easier accommodation of modern science within his biblical–theological heritage. Perhaps his interest in hypnosis and psychology focused his intensity upon human personality and the desire to make his works of practical usefulness. He appears to have found comfort in certain themes, to have reused them and refined them. What found its way into publication as *Natural Law in the Spiritual*

---

[50] Smith, *Drummond*, p. 130.

[51] Mark James Toone, "Evangelicalism in Transition: A Comparative Analysis of the Work and Theology of D. L. Moody and His Proteges, Henry Drummond and R. A. Torrey" (Ph.D. dissertation, St. Andrews University, 1988), p. 172.

[52] Nicoll, *The British Weekly*, March 18, 1897, p. 1.

World had been tried on the Philomathic Society at New College, Edinburgh, in 1873.[53] His messages later issued as Christmas booklets, such as *The Greatest Thing in the World*, *The Changed Life*, etc., according to George Adam Smith, were re-works of messages that dated back to his days as a 23-year-old helper of Moody and Sankey in their campaign of 1874–1875.[54] During the few months in 1876 that Drummond served as associate pastor of the Barclay Church in Edinburgh, he delivered the majority of the addresses that were later published posthumously in *The Ideal Life* in 1897.[55] In 1883, helping Moody and Sankey in their second British campaign, Drummond had used such apparently recycled messages as "Temptation," "The Programme of Christianity," "Seek Ye First the Kingdom of God," etc.[56]

But he was not above admitting his own limits. In one instance, when he was invited to address a large and prestigious audience, he wrote: "I have the time and the will; what fails is the theme. I can find no 'message' in my soul. . . . I never 'stuck' before for want of a subject."[57]

Natural Law in the Spiritual World came out quietly with a first impression of 1,000 copies in April of 1883, just before Drummond left on his scientific expedition to Central Africa.[58] A second edition of 1,000 came in July, but it was an impressive review in *Spectator* magazine of August 4, 1883 that brought enormous attention to the young author, inspiring sales and translation into several foreign languages. The *Spectator* allowed that except for Dr. Mozley's volume, *University Sermons*, "we can recall no book of our time which showed such power of restating the moral and practical truths of religion, so as to make them take fresh hold of the mind, and vividly impress the imagination."[59]

[53] Drummond, *New Evangelism*, p. 191.

[54] Smith, *Drummond*, p. 94.

[55] James Y. Simpson, Introductory Note in *The Ideal Life and Other Unpublished Addresses*, by Henry Drummond (London, 1897), p. 52.

[56] Lennox, *Drummond*, pp. 63–64.

[57] Simpson, *Drummond*, p. 72.

[58] Ibid., p. 60.

[59] Lennox, *Drummond*, pp. 72–73.

The instant celebrity awaiting his return from months in Africa was unanticipated by the young author whose *Natural Law* manuscript had earlier suffered several publishers' rejections. Once he had even sought to entice a publisher, claiming that with his extensive acquaintances a printing of 1,000 copies would not likely result in a loss.[60] After all, portions of the book had appeared as articles in the periodical *The Clerical World,* and the author had been offered 40 British pounds for the exclusive rights to those articles.[61]

Drummond's initial effort at book authorship was a trailblazing attempt to bring science and religion together, when science, especially among evangelicals, was detested, if not feared, as an enemy. As Nicoll has described the thought milieu of Drummond's time: "He saw that the age was essentially scientific. He saw that there appeared to be between science and religion a spanless and fathomless abyss. He discerned that the materialists were swiftly poisoning the nation and that they were following Comte in erecting materialism into a religious system."[62] In his Journal, Drummond stated his purpose in writing *Natural Law:* "If it can be shown that Christianity is scientific, i.e., that its main laws are the scientific laws only in a higher domain, the sceptic is completely silenced."[63] While *Natural Law* was sharply criticized in many quarters, at least the book provoked comment, putting the young writer's name on the lips of most of the public. As one modern writer put it, "He was Moody's man-with-a-microscope, . . . not only an evangelistic scientist, but a scientific evangelist."[64] His *Tropical Africa* (1886) is well-written and demonstrates a prodigious power of observation. Its descriptions of insects, geological formations, and cultural settings made it a useful book and gave him a certain status in the scientific world.

[60] Ibid., p. 73.
[61] Ibid., pp. 73–74.
[62] Nicholl, *The British Weekly,* March 18, 1897, pp. 1–2.
[63] Toone, "Evangelicalism in Transition," p. 172.
[64] James R. Moore, "Evangelicals and Evolution," *Scottish Journal of Theology* 38 (1985): 393.

His advice concerning student meetings, based on his experience with the student meetings at the University of Edinburgh, affords insight into his own approach to substantive thought. Drummond advised, "We never touched perplexing questions. We allowed every man to think as he liked. We respected honest doubt in every direction. Our creed was very simple. We had no creed. We had a Person. . . . Our Gospel was, 'Save your lives!' – not so much 'Save your souls!' as 'Save your lives!'. . ."[65]

His Christmas booklets, including *The Greatest Thing in the World,* are well-crafted essays that the author presented over and again, over a period of years, probably constantly revising. Nicoll wrote that ". . . Drummond could do well at once; . . . but that never led him to omit pains. His MSS. were more corrected than any that have ever passed through my hands."[66] Lennox quotes a Drummond contemporary, "It was a sight to see him revise a manuscript, correcting and correcting, as if he never could satisfy himself. He would spend half an hour over an adjective."[67]

The sketchy lineage of *The Greatest Thing in the World* reveals the repeated use, revision and improvement of "pet" themes. Apparently, *The Greatest Thing,* as well as several other essays destined to become well-known, were first given during Drummond's work with the Moody–Sankey crusade of 1874–1875.[68] Smith noted that "he had the opportunity, so invaluable to the young preacher, of giving the same addresses again and again, so that he could sift and balance them. . . ."[69] *The Greatest Thing* was published officially in 1887, at the urging of D. L. Moody, after Drummond had presented it at Moody's "Summer School for College Students" at Northfield, Massachusetts. It was entitled, "Love – The Supreme Gift."[70] Moody had first heard the love

---

[65] Shanks, ed., *A College of Colleges,* pp. 230–231.
[66] Letter, W. Robertson Nicoll to Dr. Marcus Dods, March 16, 1897.
[67] Lennox, *Drummond,* p. 146.
[68] Ibid., p. 94.
[69] Ibid., p. 94.
[70] Henry Drummond, "Love – The Supreme Gift," in Shanks, ed., *A College of Colleges,* pp. 124–142, 19.

message in June of 1884, at the conclusion of his second campaign in Britain.[71] At the Free Church at Dumfries, during Moody's second campaign in 1883, written reference was made to Drummond's "marvellous address on 'Love,' from I Cor. xiii."[72] In their memoirs, Lord and Lady Aberdeen expressed the belief that Drummond had first delivered his message on love in Haddo House Chapel and, while they suggested no date, Lord Aberdeen met Drummond in 1874, in conjunction with the Moody meetings but, as a couple, they did not actually make Drummond's acquaintance until May of 1884.[73] In August of 1884, gathered with old school chums in their annual reunion, Drummond's dear friend, Robert Barbour wrote: "He [Drummond] spoke to us tonight on Paul's Hymn of Heavenly Love in the thirteenth of First Corinthians, and it was like being in heaven or in sight of it to hear him."[74]

His appeal

Of all commentary about Henry Drummond, none is more arresting than attempts to describe his character, personality and appeal – all struggling to identify a certain mysterious distinction, a quiet charisma. In one way or another, friends' and acquaintances' views were similar to a writer's perception that "He had a mysterious aloofness that made one feel he had a world of his own into which none could quite enter."[75]

Simpson wrote:

Still, though so engaging, no one was more elusive, and consequently more difficult to portray. . . . You were conscious of an air of personal distinction that made it impossible to confound him with another. This atmosphere of distinction enveloped the man and all he did,

[71] W. R. Moody, *The Life of Dwight L. Moody*, pp. 306, 309.

[72] Lennox, *Drummond*, p. 64.

[73] Lord and Lady Aberdeen, *We Twa*, pp. 203–205.

[74] Smith, *Drummond*, p. 251.

[75] Ralph Connor, *The British Weekly*, 1903, quoted in Denis Duncan, Afterword in *The Greatest Thing in the World* by Henry Drummond (London, 1980), p. 57.

and yet it is not as if he consciously tried to be unlike his fellows, for he was the most natural of men. In it those magnetic forces that differently appealed to different individuals found a wide field. A whole series of them came into play around the hidden power of his personality. . . . Back of everything was the inexpressible sense of a man who had power with God and had prevailed.[76]

Smith sought to describe "the nameless radiance that surrounded him as of a fresh spring morning – but, indeed, it is his biographer's despair to explain to those who never felt it the equal charm and force which came out from him."[77] "He was one of the purest, most unselfish, most reverent souls you ever knew; but you would not have called him saint. The name he went by among younger men was 'The Prince'; there was a distinction and a radiance upon him that compelled the title."[78]

Even among his colleagues, Drummond seemed to reflect special standing. Lilian Adam Smith, wife of Drummond's principal biographer, in her own memoirs quoted a Glasgow professor, contemporary of Drummond and of her husband, J. L. Morrison, who wrote her decades after Drummond's death: ". . . Henry Drummond, surely the most striking to hear and see of any professors of his time, with all the distinction attaching to his books and his remarkable evangelistic work. . . ."[79]

That special sense of distinction seems to have been apparent even from childhood. John Watson, his boyhood friend, described his first meeting Drummond on a cricket field when they were barely teenagers, and wrote:

> In my boyish and dull mind I had a sense that he was a type by himself, a visitor of finer breed than those among whom he moved. . . . What impressed me that pleasant evening in the days of long ago I can now identify. It was the lad's distinction, an inherent quality of appearance and manner of character and soul which marked him and made him solitary. What happened with one strange lad that evening befell all kinds of people who met

[76] Simpson, *Drummond*, pp. 147–148.
[77] Smith, *Drummond*, p. 95.
[78] Ibid., p. 3.
[79] Lilian Adam Smith, *George Adam Smith*, p. 112.

Drummond in later years. They were at once arrested, interested, fascinated by the very sight of the man, and could not take their eyes off him. . . . One did not realize how commonplace and colourless other men were till they stood side by side with Drummond. Upon a platform of evangelists, or sitting among divinity students in a dingy classroom, or cabined in the wooden respectability of an ecclesiastical court, or standing in a crowd of passengers at a railway station, he suggested golden embroidery upon hodden gray. It was as if the prince of one's imagination had dropped in among common folk. He reduced us all to the peasantry.[80]

"His was a personality indeed – no man was ever mistaken for Drummond, nor was he ever mistaken for any other."[81]

To reach back over the years seeking to parse that special charisma seems fruitless. However, contributing features seem to include his good looks and bearing, his striking eyes, his selflessness and interest in others, sincerity and a thoughtful choice of words. Almost everyone who wrote about Drummond referenced his personal attractiveness, his dapper dress and personal style that set him apart. Smith wrote of ". . .The tall, lithe figure, the keen eyes, the unstrained voice, the imperturbable spirit, the purity and earnestness which were behind all."[82] A college lecturer, who remembered hearing Drummond at Edinburgh while a medical student (1888–1892), wrote that "He was admittedly a tall, well-built, handsome man – almost a king among men. . . . He was rather particularly well and neatly dressed."[83] "On the street, his well-set-up form, his erect carriage, his 'princely swing' as someone has called it, his faultless attire, differentiated him from every other member of the passing crowd." Lennox pictured Drummond on a platform, "attired in a well-cut frock coat, closely buttoned, and wearing a particular shape of collar, and a quiet-coloured necktie."[84]

[80] Watson, "Memorial Sketch," pp. 25–27.
[81] Lennox, *Drummond*, p. 99.
[82] Smith, *Drummond*, p. 95.
[83] Ibid., p. 329.
[84] Lennox, *Drummond*, pp. 99–100.

In 1885, a contemporary newspaperman who attended Drummond's by-invitation-only meetings of London's highest society at Grosvenor House, London residence of the Duke of Westminster, reported that ". . . the audience has departed profoundly impressed by the words of wisdom and solemnity issuing from the lips of a young man with a good manner, a not ill-favoured face, a broad Scotch accent, clad in a remarkably well-fitting frock coat. . . ."[85]

By all accounts, the unique and commanding feature of his face was his eye. "No photograph could do it justice, and very often photographs have done it injustice, by giving the idea of staringness. His eye was not bold or fierce; it was tender and merciful. But it had power and hold which were little else than irresistible and almost supernatural."[86] As the student George Newman recalled, ". . . no one who has looked into those eyes can ever hold any other opinion than that they were attractive."[87] His three principal biographers commented: "The keen brown eyes got at your heart, and you felt you could speak your best to them."[88] "You were held by the deep-set, thoughtful, tender eyes. . . ."[89] Lennox noted that boys of the Brigade "simply adored him" and were always inclined to comment on Drummond's wonderful eyes.[90] His friend, Watson, remembered: "When you talked with Drummond he did not look at you and out of the window alternately, as is the usual manner, he never moved his eyes and gradually their penetrating gaze seemed to reach and encompass your soul."[91]

A contemporary newspaper observed: "He has a charm of manner and an electricity of eye which fascinate. When conversing with you he gives you the impression that he is intensely interested in *you* of all men. This power, carried into his public speaking,

---

[85] Smith, *Drummond*, p. 257.
[86] Watson, "Memorial Sketch," p. 27.
[87] Smith, *Drummond*, p. 329.
[88] Ibid., p. 3.
[89] Simpson, *Drummond*, p. 148.
[90] Lennox, *Drummond*, p. 186.
[91] Watson, "Drummond," p. 516.

gives him the wonderful hold over his audience which he possesses."[92]

With his gift of friendship, Drummond easily focused on others, but was curiously independent of them. In fact, as Smith noted: "The longer you knew him, the fact which most impressed you was that he seldom talked about himself, and, no matter how deep the talk might go, never about that inner self. . . ."[93] "Many confidences he must have received; he gave none. . . ."[94] "He himself did not ask for sympathy, and did not seem to need it. The innermost secrets of his life were between himself and his Saviour."[95] Simpson mentions that many people found in Drummond a certain "loneliness or aloofness that was seemingly inexplicable."[96]

Style and delivery

Fastidious about the use of language, Drummond had "very unusual endowments as an orator and as a writer. No one we have ever listened to impressed us quite in the same way. His words were the effortless utterance of a man with a message, a man who could clothe his thoughts in the simplest and at the same time the most shining vesture."[97] Yet he was conscious of the risk he took with his independence and his public candor. Drummond wrote ". . . A public man takes his life in his hands every time he opens his lips. . . . He is liable to have his influence marred and his mind troubled for years by any spark of suspicion regarding him that may be idly dropped on the combustible elements of religious intolerance."[98]

Drummond's propensity for rewriting and editing his work was lifelong. He once said that a magazine article should be written

[92] *Glasgow Evening News*, March 11, 1897.
[93] Smith, *Drummond*, p. 4.
[94] Watson, "Drummond," p. 519.
[95] Nicoll, "Memorial Sketch," p. 2.
[96] Simpson, *Drummond*, p. 152.
[97] Nicoll, *The British Weekly*, March 18, 1897, p. 1.
[98] Lennox, *Drummond*, p. 160.

at least three times – "once in simplicity, once in profundity, and once to make the profundity appear simplicity."[99] Nicoll, himself an editor, noted that "everything he published was elaborated with the most scrupulous care. I have never seen manuscripts so carefully revised as his."[100]

Reference has been made to the mesmeric effect Drummond had on his hearers. Nicoll believed that ". . . more than most other speakers we have ever listened to he has the power of arresting attention and holding the audience spellbound from the first word to the last. This, however, is accomplished altogether without noise or trick of rhetoric, by the fascination of the man and the freshness of his message."[101]

Yet his style of speaking was "simple and clear. . . ."[102] It does not appear that he had any special training in elocution or oratory as could be obtained in the Scotland of his day. He apparently was deliberate in seeking a conversational tone and not to fit into normal ministerial mannerisms.

As a speaker, he identified with his listener. Stalker has said that Drummond "went as far as conscience would allow, in order to meet the doubter and the man of the world on their own ground."[103] He was conscious of the special nature of the audience of university students. Advising a Northfield crowd on how to address university students, Drummond said: "There is nothing a student hates so much as cant. By cant I simply mean anything that is unnatural, false, falsetto, untrue to experience – anything that is sentimental or sanctimonious – anything in the shape of exaggerated expression or exaggerated emotion."[104]

While he prized originality and freshness, Drummond had almost an aversion to cleverness of speech and to emotion. In sharing before Moody's Northfield audience his approach to the Edinburgh student meetings, Drummond explained what they were looking

---

[99] Ibid., p. 146.
[100] Nicoll, "Memorial Sketch," p. 18.
[101] *The British Weekly*, March 18, 1897, p. 2.
[102] Smith, *Drummond*, p. 95.
[103] Lennox, *Drummond*, p. 106.
[104] Shanks, ed., *A College of Colleges*, p. 229.

for in persons to go out on "deputation" teams. "The one dis-qualification for going on a deputation was eloquence and fluency. If a man could talk easily, he was immediately dropped. If a man used fine phrases he was sent about his business. What we wanted was facts – facts in their simplest form. . . ."[105]

But he worked diligently to avoid cliches in self-expression. He told an American audience:

> Other men are kept away from Christianity by what I might call its phrases. A great many people, not so much in your country as in ours, talk in a dialect. The older people especially, our grand-mothers, have a set of phrases in which all their religion is imbedded, and they can't talk to us about religion without using those phrases. . . .[106]

With all the factors we can retrospectively bring into focus, we can celebrate anew the personal devotion and unique success of Henry Drummond. He was a chosen servant who was faithful in a most unconventional way. Perhaps as fine a tribute as can be recognized, looking back over his life and the years since his death, is to read again the splendid praises of his close friends. In our age when close friendships are less common and almost suspect, it is touching to re-create the scene described by one of D. L. Moody's biographers, who wrote: "On hearing of Drummond's untimely death at forty-five in 1897 Moody at Goss' house in Cincinnati cried like a child. 'He was the most Christlike man I ever met. I never saw a fault in him,' he said over and over again through his sobs."[107]

[105] Ibid., p. 232.
[106] Henry Drummond, *Stones Rolled Away* (New York, 1899), p. 17.
[107] J. C. Pollock, *Moody: A Biographical Portrait of the Pacesetter in Modern Mass Evangelism* (New York, 1963), p. 302.

Henry Drummond in America: A Centennial Celebration

5

❧❧❀❧❧

Henry Drummond:
from Scotland to America
with love

Thomas E. and Marla Haas Corts

On three trips to America during a short lifetime of 45 years, Henry Drummond found this young nation brash, rambunctious and exhilarating. When he was only 27 and this nation had just celebrated its centennial, his first visit to America in 1879 introduced him to the rugged life of the developing West, the magnificence of the Grand Canyon, the bustling ambition of developing cities. Musing after his return, he wrote: "The whole of America impresses me now as a *revelation* – a revelation in civilisation, in politics, in human nature; and if not a revelation in geology, a confirmation, elevation and consolidation, which is more than equivalent."[1] Later he wrote that in America he felt as if he were taking "a bath of life" and more than once he said that "a nation in its *youth* was a stirring spectacle."[2]

The people of this country were more than equally enthralled with the young Scot, whose three peripatetic adventures in America

---

[1] Letter, Drummond to Professor Archibald Geikie, November 22, 1879, quoted in George Adam Smith, *The Life of Henry Drummond*, 2nd ed. (London, 1899), p. 175.

[2] Cuthbert Lennox [J. H. Napier], *Henry Drummond: A Biographical Sketch*, 4th ed. (London, 1902), p. 121.

– in 1879, 1887, and 1893 – came at a time when the Lyceum movement was strong, and the traveling lecturer was in great demand, peddling world perspectives and great ideas to common persons in small towns and large. By the time of his second visit, Drummond was probably more appreciated in America than in his own country. From Harvard, Yale and Princeton to the upstart University of Chicago, by the time of the 1887 and 1893 visits, America's universities and other institutions recognized Drummond's intellectual celebrity. Drummond called Boston "the hub of the universe" and "the great centre of literary life in America,"[3] and even staid Boston was admiring, with one local publication claiming in 1893 that of all significant events then stirring religious circles, "the presence in the city for two months of Professor Henry Drummond" was second only to the death of Phillips Brooks.[4] In fact, the Rev. C. K. O. Spence, long time pastor, now retired, of the Drummond Memorial Church in Glasgow, queried in a letter to Eric Motley just this past summer: "Why has all the interest about H. D. come from outside of his native Scotland? Wherefore Scotland's lukewarm recognition of the man?"[5]

A brief overview of Drummond's status may serve well at this point. He was, of course, a Professor of Natural Science in a minister-training college (seminary), the Free Church College, Glasgow. The strangeness of a science professor in a seminary is explained by the fact that science was not included in the University requirements of that era, and the wisdom of the Church of Scotland was that the ministry should not be ignorant of science, whether for preaching material or for reasons of apologetics.[6] So, with science in its ministerial-training curriculum, an uncommon professor was needed – a science-minded minister or a minister-minded scientist – and Henry Drummond was such a man. He succeeded

[3] Quotation from Drummond's Journal in Lennox, *Drummond*, p. 117.

[4] The undated quotation is from Howard Bridgman, *The Boston Congrega-tionalist*, 1893, in the Drummond Papers, National Library of Scotland.

[5] Letter, Spence to Motley, July 31, 1997; Spence raised the same question of me in a Letter, Spence to Corts, April 17, 1998.

[6] Smith, *Drummond*, pp. 119–120.

the deceased Mr. Keddie, a long-term holder of the same lecture-ship, by accepting a temporary appointment for 1877–1878, at 100 or 150 pounds per year for four lectures a week, November through March.[7] Drummond was a spiritually-minded man who did not fit contemporary religious conventions, had made quite a name for himself as a helper to Moody, had completed theological training, had been very interested in science, and who had the strong endorsement of the esteemed Professor Geikie. Throughout his life, Drummond saw himself as an evangelist. (In fact, while he came to be addressed most often as "Professor Drummond," in Britain's polite, title-conscious society, he once said the title "evangelist" suited him best.)[8]

Though he had functioned as a minister, Henry Drummond did not consider himself a cleric and resisted ordination as long as he could. Finally, in 1884, when ordination was required for appointment to an endowed chair at Free Church College, he submitted – though even thereafter he considered himself *not* to have been ordained to the ministry, *per se*. Almost with a twinkle in his eye, he would later claim to have no remembrance of ordination, and he corrected correspondents inclined to address him as "Reverend."[9] After his appointment at the Free Church College, he appeared to make a point of not preaching. For example, in a letter responding to a preaching invitation, he wrote in his

[7] Smith, *Drummond*, p. 120. While Smith stated that Drummond's salary was 150 pounds, an extract from the records of the College Committee, September 18, 1877, among the Drummond Papers, states that he be appointed "interim lecturer" and "that an allowance of 100 pounds be made to Mr. Drummond for his services."

[8] Observations about a proper title for Drummond were not infrequent. "Professor" seems to have won out in common usage. In the Drummond Papers at the University of Glasgow I recall seeing a report quoting Drummond as saying that he preferred the title "evangelist."

[9] Considerable confusion has existed over whether Drummond was actually ordained. An excellent discussion of the technicalities, concluding that he was first ordained as an elder, and then, in fact, fully ordained, is in Smith, *Drummond*, pp. 245–246; Lennox, *Drummond*, p. 53; Drummond explains himself on the subject in a letter to friends in 1879; see Smith, *Drummond*, pp. 125–126.

own hand: "I never preach – cannot. Least of all could I attempt Anniversary Services."[10]

However, writing his mother from America (August 21, 1879), Drummond detailed at least one ministerial service that afforded a perspective on the rougher side of young America. He was standing in the doorway of a hotel in Boulder, Colorado, "a new gold-mining district right up among the mountains." A man came up, excitedly asking the landlord where a minister lived, as a miner had died about ten miles away in a lonely canyon, and they wanted to provide a proper burial. Drummond volunteered that if they could not find a minister, he would go. An hour later the man reappeared to claim Drummond's offer of last resort, and Drummond "in his tweeds," found a white tie at a nearby store which, he stated, "gave one quite a sufficient professional look for the mountains." He ended up with an impressive experience among a multinational, immigrant audience he described as "kindly, brave, but wild and lawless." He reflected that it had been a "golden opportunity" for evangelism and that it might be years before there was another service in that camp, "as it is one of the loneliest inhabited spots on earth."[11]

Henry Drummond first laid eyes on America in August, 1879, invited by his old Professor, Sir Archibald Geikie, to join an expedition into Western North America to study "volcanic phenomena." Geikie explained, "Desiring a companion, I at once turned to my favourite pupil and found him willing to join me."[12]

---

[10] Letter, Drummond to Mrs. Malheron, July 13, 1885. Drummond seems to have taken this position, even though he had preached at the church station at Malta three times a Sunday during the summer of 1878 (Smith, *Drummond*, p. 122). In 1877, he had assisted the minister of Barclay Church with responsibility for sermon preparation (Smith, *Drummond*, p. 113). He began a four-year pastorship of the Possil Park mission of Renfield Free Church in April, 1878, writing to friends that "On Sunday, I preach twice. . . ." (Letter, Drummond to Mr. and Mrs. Stuart, November 22, 1878, quoted in Smith, *Drummond*, p. 125). See also Lennox, *Drummond*, p. 56.

[11] Letter, Drummond to his mother, August 21, 1879; Smith, *Drummond*, pp. 155–156.

[12] Reminiscence of Geikie, written to G. A. Smith, in Smith, *Drummond*, p. 153.

In the month of preparation, the two exchanged letters discussing camping equipment and expressing concern about the "unsettled condition of the Indians in the Rocky Mountains."[13] Smith stated that Drummond used to speak of the great generosity of the U.S. government, which provided the geologists with an escort of soldiers, their supplies, and letters of introduction.[14] For two months, the Geikie party wandered the West, making notes of distinctive rock formations, taking in the wonder of the scenery, marveling at the prairies, the sport of wildlife and fishing, observing the native Indians.[15]

At the end of the western expedition, Henry was in Boston with one week to himself before departing for home. Testifying to the bonds of friendship, Drummond gave up the opportunity to have dinner in Boston with Oliver Wendell Holmes and Henry Wadsworth Longfellow, whom he greatly admired, in order to travel 800 miles each way by train to be with his old friends Moody and Sankey who were conducting mission work in Cleveland, Ohio.[16] He had first met the American evangelists in Scotland in 1873–1874 when, as local ministerial students, their help was enlisted. Though not 23 years old at the time, Drummond took on great responsibility for follow-up to the Moody–Sankey crusade and became a valued friend of the Americans.

It was on that 800-mile trip that Drummond recorded a strange experience. He said:

> Some 50 miles, perhaps – before reaching the city [Cleveland], the train slowed somewhat, and I observed two gentlemen in the next compartment look with a sudden interest out of the window at the

[13] Smith, *Drummond*, p. 154.

[14] Ibid., p. 154.

[15] J. Y. Simpson, *Henry Drummond* (Edinburgh, 1901), p. 102, notes that among his wild west experiences, Drummond never forgot the sensation of finding himself confronted and fully covered by Indian rifles, pending an exchange of mutual assurances of friendship.

[16] Smith, *Drummond*, pp. 127–128. On his 1887 visit to America he visited with Mark Twain and Mrs. Harriet Beecher Stowe, according to a letter in the Drummond Papers. In 1893, he visited with Holmes; see Smith, *Drummond*, p. 499.

left. I followed their example instinctively, and found that we were rolling along a high viaduct which spanned a dark ravine. At one end lay a small pile of newly dressed stones, as if the bridge had been recently repaired. The thought seized me somehow that I knew this place, that I had seen it in words or a picture at some former period. And then the impression came with the speed of lightning, and I found myself saying, "Yes, this is it – the fatal bridge – the spot where P. P. Bliss was translated in a chariot of fire." I had not the most remote idea that among the tens of thousands of miles of railroad on that vast continent, I was traveling over the particular spot which embalms that tragic memory. . . . I learned from Mr. Sankey without any surprise, some hours later, of its correctness. The place was Ashtabula.[17]

P. P. Bliss was the well-respected American hymn-writer, who had worked with Moody and Sankey in America. Among his hymns were: "Hold the Fort," "Almost Persuaded," "It Is Well With My Soul" (words only), "The Light of the World Is Jesus." Since Bliss's death in the train accident occurred in 1876 and he had not been to England, he probably never met Drummond. However, Moody and Sankey had no doubt told Drummond about Bliss, and Bliss's hymns had been used extensively in Britain, and were included in the famous Sankey songbook which sold hundreds of thousands of copies in Britain during the 1870s and 1880s. *En route* via train from Buffalo, New York to Chicago, a 159-foot train trestle gave way in heavy snow seventy-five feet above a ravine in Ashtabula, Ohio, and Bliss and his wife were killed along with 100 other passengers.[18]

In Cleveland, surprises awaited the young Scot, eager to compare Moody–Sankey meetings in Cleveland with those in Britain. Though he had not seen the evangelistic team for five years, he had anticipated that their rigorous schedule might have left "traces somehow marked upon their frames." But he saw Moody

---

[17] Henry Drummond, "A Visit to Mr. Moody and Mr. Sankey," *New Zealand Christian Record* (1880).

[18] The "Ashtabula Bridge Disaster," including contemporary newspaper accounts, is described more fully in D. W. Whittle, ed., *Memoirs of Philip P. Bliss* (New York, 1877).

and Sankey "not changed by a hair's breadth – the same men:
Mr. Sankey, down to the faultless set of his black neck-tie; Mr.
Moody, to the chronic crush of his collar."[19] The tone and tenor
of the meetings also surprised him.

> It was the same as England and Scotland. I was especially pleased
> to find that it was the same as regards *quietness*. I had expected to
> find revival work in America more exciting; but although a deep
> work was beginning, everything was calm. There was movement
> but no agitation; there was power in the meetings but no frenzy.
> And the secret of that probably lay here, that in the speaker himself
> there was earnestness but no bigotry, and enthusiasm but no
> superstition. . . .[20]

So the first visit to America was a wild west geological expedition
in companionship with his scientific mentor, Geikie, capped off
with the fellowship of his evangelism mentors, Moody and Sankey.
He had seen America, from camping out in the canyons and prairies
of the West, cavalry escorts and confrontations with Indians,
rugged, frontier mining towns, to polite Boston society and warm
Midwest evangelicalism.

Henry Drummond's second visit to America came in 1887. It
is unclear what originally prompted the trip but two invitations
were the likely impetus. Having heard for the first time in 1884
Drummond's impressive oral essay on I Corinthians 13, Moody
was determined not to rest until he brought Drummond to
Northfield to deliver that address; so Drummond was scheduled
for the Northfield, Massachusetts student conference. A second
invitation was that of Amherst College, which had elected to
confer upon Drummond an honorary doctorate at Commencement June 25, 1887. (It was the only degree he ever had.)[21]
But the 35-year-old Henry Drummond who arrived in America
June 18, 1887 was different than on his first visit in 1879, when

[19] Lennox, *Drummond*, p. 188.
[20] Ibid., pp. 118–119.
[21] The archives of Amherst College include a Commencement Program with
Drummond's name listed. Smith, *Drummond*, p. 420; Lennox, *Drummond*, p.
123.

he was only 27. He had compressed intense experience into the intervening eight years – having endured a mentally and physically rigorous trip into the interior of Africa, having found worldwide fame as the best-selling author of an attention-getting book, and having stirred the leading university in his homeland with a special work that was making a mark on university and medical students.

The year 1884 stands out as one great year in Henry Drummond's life. Arriving home that Spring from ten months almost incommunicado in deepest Africa, he stepped from darkness into the brilliant light of sudden fame. His book, *Natural Law in the Spiritual World*, had been released by the publisher just as he set sail and unknown to him, during his self-exile to Africa, it became a publishing success[22] in England and America. He had gone off to Africa a locally-known young professor. He returned to find himself the subject of newspaper reviews, cartoon drawings, and controversy.[23] In an even more serious way, he was also changed by the severe experience of Africa. While he had begun the journey with a sense of boyish adventure as "one continuous picnic from first to last," for ten months, Drummond lived a physically and emotionally arduous existence in jungle and bush, secluded, with limited mail his tenuous and irregular connection to the outside world.[24] To that time, every white birth in Central Africa had cost a mother's life.[25] The only two British children in the land died while he was up country.[26] He suffered his own bout of lassitude and fever, spending days in his tent under unremitting rain, a month of weakness and inertia. He witnessed firsthand the horrors of the slave trade with the traders' paths marked by human bones and human heads impaled on the posts of their prison

---

[22] Lennox, *Drummond*, p. 73.

[23] Lennox notes (*Drummond*, p. 74) that twenty-one books and pamphlets were issued in English criticizing *Natural Law in the Spiritual World*, soon after its publication, and Drummond appeared with other prominent authors in a cartoon drawing in *Punch*, March 28, 1885.

[24] Smith, *Drummond*, pp. 209–211.

[25] Ibid., p. 210.

[26] Ibid., p. 210.

stockades.[27] Back in England, he told a friend, "I've been in an atmosphere of death all the time."[28] As George Adam Smith, his friend and biographer relates: ". . . from 1884 onwards there came upon his always pure and sympathetic temper a certain tinge of sadness with which we had not been able to associate him in previous years."[29]

In addition to his return from Africa (survival may have been triumph enough), and his sudden burst of fame as an author, the visit of C. T. Studd and Stanley Smith to the University of Edinburgh was the other event of 1884 that was to have profound consequences for Drummond. Out of that visit came the invitation for Drummond to address the Sunday night meetings that made such a profound impression upon the student community and gave Drummond such an important outlet for his brand of evangelism.[30]

So, his second visit to America was as a widely-known author and world traveler, and the press followed his movement around the country.[31] Drummond was at Amherst to receive his honorary degree, and though older and wiser, at 35 he was one of the youngest

[27] The horrors of slave traders is characterized by Drummond as "the heart disease of Africa," which he discusses in Chapter IV of his *Tropical Africa*, 1888. Smith, *Drummond*, p. 210.

[28] Smith, *Drummond*, p. 211.

[29] Ibid., p. 211.

[30] Simpson, *Drummond*, pp. 63–64. The amazing ministry of Stanley Smith and C. T. Studd was told by Drummond to the students at Moody's Northfield Student Conference in 1887 and recorded in T. J. Shanks, ed., *A College of Colleges: Led by D. L. Moody* (Chicago, 1887), pp. 228–229. The story of Smith and Studd, as well as the others of their era who came to be known as "The Cambridge Seven," is chronicled by J. C. Pollock, *The Cambridge Seven* (London, 1955). See, also, Norman Grubb, *C. T. Studd: Cricketer and Pioneer*, 1933.

[31] Drummond was never a fan of the American press. In one letter, he wrote: "I have been 'interviewed' several times, but some of the accounts I have never seen, and others are so absurd that I have been ashamed to send them to you. . . ." (Smith, *Drummond*, p. 346). Drummond described to a reporter, "The Americans have made me shy of journalists. In whatever strict privacy I might think I was delivering an address, it would shortly be reported – and alas! reported in a way that made it altogether unrecognizable to me – the next day" (*The Christian Herald*, March 25, 1897).

persons ever to receive an honorary doctorate there. He proceeded to Moody's conference at Northfield, Massachusetts by June 28, where it was noted that "Professor Henry Drummond, of Scotland, was the most notable figure among the many eminent speakers by whom Mr. Moody was surrounded."[32] Departing Northfield to visit his dear friends, Lord and Lady Aberdeen at Niagara, on their way home from India, he traveled on to a local Chautauqua at South Framingham, Massachusetts, and the original Chautauqua in New York state.[33] From there, he went to speak at Greenfield, Massachusetts and on to New York City for the meeting of the American Association for the Advancement of Science.[34] With the American academic year starting in September, he had abundant invitations. But it was risky to think American collegians would be interested in Drummond and in his account of the student work going on at Edinburgh. He had already lectured to large crowds at Oxford, but would America be the same? He had written to the Aberdeens about his Oxford visit:

> When I got to Trinity, I found the hall so crammed that we could scarcely get in. All the passages were crowded, all the tables, forms, cornices, and window sills, with a seething mass of undergraduates. The door being blocked, they were forcing in through the windows and filling every inch of space. I need not say how inspiring this sight was. It was a most unconventional and picturesque audience, the sort I like best.[35]

So, in the fall of 1887, his freshly-minted doctorate in hand, Drummond embarked on a campus circuit at a furious pace to Williams College, Dartmouth College, Amherst again; then in early October, to Yale, Princeton, Harvard and Wellesley, and among the medical students of New York City. In each place he

---

[32] Shanks, ed., *A College of Colleges*, p. 20.

[33] Smith, *Drummond*, pp. 343–345.

[34] Smith, *Drummond*, pp. 347–348. Drummond lectured "mostly on African insects" to a very prestigious audience that included "all the savants of the country" (Smith, *Drummond*, p. 348).

[35] Lord and Lady Aberdeen, *We Twa: Reminiscences of Lord and Lady Aberdeen*, 2 vols. (London, 1925), Vol. I, p. 207.

did a little evangelizing, but he also told of the especially effective ministry to students that had begun at the University of Edinburgh. (As he explained them, they were simple Sunday night meetings, with a hymn, a prayer, and then a message – all quite calm and unemotional, but it seemed to have uncommon power in its effect upon young university men and particularly medical students.)[36]

The proprietor of a lecture bureau, touting himself as one who had arranged speaking tours for such notables as Matthew Arnold, Henry Stanley, and Charles Dickens, wrote offering Drummond $5,000 to give fifty lectures, starting in October.[37] An American who heard Drummond at Chautauqua said that "many English lights have been envious of American gold" but not Drummond.[38] Offered $100 after lecturing at Clifton Springs, New York, Drummond impressed the people in charge by taking only enough to get to his next venue.[39] He wrote home that he had been invited to be principal of colleges, to write for newspapers, "to lecture in half the states of the Union, and otherwise to line my pockets with dollars."[40] But as always, Drummond seemed resistant to personal gain.

What particularly moved Drummond was the prospect of sharing with American campuses the type of student meetings and student evangelism that enjoyed such success at the University of Edinburgh. He had been joined in September of 1887 by several of his co-workers in the Edinburgh student effort, two faculty members and two students, and this appears now to have been the first direct appeal for Christian student work on the college/university campus. *The Williams Weekly* reported that Professor Drummond was "so widely known as the author of *Natural Law in the Spiritual World*," and that at all of the services "there was a

[36] Drummond in Shanks, ed., *A College of Colleges*, pp. 237–238.

[37] The offer was from James B. Pond, proprietor and manager of Everett House, New York, and a well-known lecture-promoter who had arranged tours for Charles Dickens, Henry Stanley, Matthew Arnold, and others. The offer is in a Letter from Pond to Drummond in the Drummond Papers.

[38] *The British Weekly*, March 18, 1897.

[39] *The British Weekly*, March 18, 1897.

[40] Smith, *Drummond*, p. 344.

large attendance, and a great deal of interest manifested. . . ." The newspaper concluded: "Their coming to this college was greatly appreciated and their departure much regretted."[41]

Two weeks later, *The Williams Weekly* summarized the impressive impact of Professor Drummond and his party at Yale. After Drummond's visit, forty or fifty students, prominent in athletics and in literary work, left Yale every Sunday to visit other institutions, meet with students and share a Christian message.[42] At Amherst College, the *Amherst Student* stated that the large audience completely filled College Church[43] to hear Professor Drummond "the central figure of the delegation, owing to the eminence which he has attained in his department, and well known through his book, '*Natural Law in the Spiritual World*'. . . ." Drummond was praised for his "straightforward methods, his freedom from all cant, his clear way of putting the truth, and apt illustrations. . . ."[44] From Amherst, a group of students was chosen to represent "the Christian element of the College" to neighboring cities of Williston and Easthampton and "to give an account of the visit of Professor Drummond and his friends from Scotland."[45]

Harvard's *The Daily Crimson* spoke of Drummond as "a man whom the University should be glad to welcome. The single book which he has written has already made him famous on both sides of the water." The editorialist counseled: "Harvard certainly ought not to be behind other colleges in readiness to listen to an earnest and scholarly Christian; a broad-minded man of today, who comes in a peculiarly friendly capacity as a delegate from the universities of the old country."[46] For his first address, Harvard's "Holden Chapel was crowded to its utmost capacity to hear Drummond tell them that he had not come to preach but to help – to try to remove the misconception in men's minds in regard to

[41] *Williams Weekly*, October 1, 1887.
[42] *Williams Weekly*, October 15, 1887.
[43] *Amherst Student*, September 28, 1887.
[44] *Amherst Student*, September 28, 1887.
[45] *Amherst Student*, September 28, 1887.
[46] *The Daily Crimson*, October 8, 1887.

Christianity." He concluded: "You, since you are Harvard students, have more influence than all the other young men in this country. If this college should become a power for Christ, it would influence the whole country. . . ."[47]

What made Drummond so appealing to students? At least three reasons may be cited. (1) The novelty of his direct appeal to students was unprecedented. "Coming to us as students they had a wonderful power of gaining the sympathies of students."[48] (2) Drummond's repute gained through his book was substantial. In a day before extensive global communication and before radio, television and movies, icons of popular culture were not yet created. Drummond was about as world famous as any religious personality of his day and created curiosity among students who recognized his fame, their campus newspapers calling him "widely-known," "famous on both sides of the water," and writing of his "eminence." (3) Drummond's willingness to tackle scientific questions and to harmonize science and Christianity was appealing to students, whose parents and ministers were all too ready to draw a distinct line between science and religion. "That the educated men of Scotland have sent across the ocean to fellow-students here such men to do such work is a matter for rumination to a large class of people still existing, who believe that science and culture are skepticism and infidelity," stated *The Williams Weekly*.[49] (4) His warmhearted reasonableness, as opposed to emotional appeals. A contemporary minister credited Drummond's effectiveness to "His youth, his ease of approach, his ability, his simplicity, his method of satisfying the reason before attempting to arouse the feelings or to move the will – appeal with special persuasiveness to college men."[50]

Two years after his American visit, he was still getting mail from American colleges and their students. One letter was from the popular Plummer Professor of Harvard, Francis Peabody, who

[47] *The Daily Crimson*, October 11, 12, 1887.
[48] *The Williams Weekly*, October 1, 1887.
[49] *The Williams Weekly*, October 1, 1887.
[50] The Reverend Charles Fleming of Minneapolis in *The Boston Congregationalist*, 1888; see also, Smith, *Drummond*, p. 356.

wrote: "I venture to recall myself to you and to report to you the substantial good that has remained of your week among us here. . . . I should very much like to meet you once more and to tell you how the religious life of our University has been led since your visit to us. . . . Meantime, pray be sure that a debt of serious obligation is still felt to you here for your wise and inspiring counsel."[51]

By the time of his 1893 visit, Drummond was 41 years of age, and even better known. The memory of his 1887 visits was still cherished among eastern colleges and universities. Lecture bureaus were still offering their enticements. His *Natural Law in the Spiritual World* had been in print almost ten years, and had sold over 100,000 copies in English, had been translated into five or six languages, and brought its author heaps of letters.[52] His meditation on I Corinthians 13, *The Greatest Thing in the World*, had first been published in America by Moody in a compendium of addresses given at his 1887 Northfield student conference, and was issued in Britain at Christmas, 1889. It had sold 185,000 copies in the first six months to "thousands . . . thirsting to make acquaintance with Drummond's charms as a religious teacher."[53] Other booklets followed, so that his fame was still in the ascendancy when he set foot in New York City, March 30, 1893.

While his primary purpose in crossing the Atlantic the third time was to give the Lowell Institute Lectures, a series started in 1839 and reserved for only an elite corps of famous scholars, artists, literary and scientific authorities, he also planned to visit Lord and Lady Aberdeen in Canada and to enjoy a Canadian fishing expedition with his friend, W. E. Dodge of New York. (Dodge's father, W. E. Dodge, Sr., after marrying the daughter of Mr. Phelps, put together the Phelps-Dodge Corporation, one of the world's premier copper mining organizations. Both W. E. Dodges were men of great wealth and tremendous dedication to the evangelical,

[51] Letter, Peabody to Drummond, May 1, 1889, quoted in Smith, *Drummond*, pp. 356–357.

[52] Smith, *Drummond*, pp. 212–213, 224.

[53] Lennox, *Drummond*, p. 147.

Christian cause.) So, Drummond was to spend all summer and fall in North America with a schedule that was by turns both hectic and recreational; yet, it was his most relaxed visit to this continent.

Immediately, he was surprised by the overwhelming appeal of his Lowell Lectures, more positive perhaps than any other recorded response to Drummond. It was estimated that for every person who attended, ten people were turned away. Disappointment at not being admitted was so strong that Drummond agreed to give each lecture a second time to a second audience. *The Boston Herald* carried accounts of each Drummond lecture and included a few sentences in the news summary on page one. Reporters repeatedly commented on the enormous crowds: "The audience was all that the hall could contain, and hundreds went away disappointed. The professor smiled as he saw the sea of faces before him, and the ladies sitting Turk fashion on the platform."[54] *The Herald* noted in its issue of April 26, that giving out tickets for the repetition of the lecture had relieved the pressure to hear him, "but the hall was, nevertheless, crowded, and not all who desired could secure seats."[55] A couple of weeks later, enthusiasm was unabated, the report stating: "Every evening sees all the seats filled and many people sent away, and the afternoon repetitions have similar audiences."[56] "The hot weather had absolutely no effect on the attendance at Prof. Drummond's lectures . . . last evening. The hall was completely filled before the professor arrived, and when he did reach the lecture hall, he found an enthusiastic audience to greet him with applause."[57]

The Lowell Lectures covered about a dozen events, spread over several weeks' time so that he took other engagements, intermittently. Having already become a conversation piece in the Boston area, Drummond was a sensation at Harvard. An editorial in *The Daily Crimson* advised in advance of his coming: "The opportunity of listening to so eminent a man as Professor Drummond is a rare one, even at Harvard, where we enjoy unusual

[54] *The Boston Herald*, April 19, 1893.
[55] *The Boston Herald*, April 26, 1893.
[56] *The Boston Herald*, May 6, 1893.
[57] *The Boston Herald*, May 13, 1893.

privileges in hearing many of the foremost thinkers of the age."[58]
One lead of a front page story reporting Drummond's lecture
complained: "Sever 11 was not nearly large enough to hold the
men who gathered to hear Professor Drummond again last night."
And, after student complaints about townspeople getting the
advantage in seating, *The Daily Crimson* editorialized:

> The scene at the entrance to Appleton Chapel last night was not
> surprising considering the intense desire to hear Professor
> Drummond. . . . It would not seem too radical a measure, then, to
> let it be known that the service next Sunday will not be open to the
> public, but only to students and those who clearly accompany them
> as friends. . . . Unless some such provision is made, we may expect
> to see even a greater crush than the one last night. . . . The public
> have been given their chance: the students now respectfully ask to
> be admitted to their own Chapel.[59]

The Boston Herald had called it "one of the largest audiences ever
assembled there at a Sunday evening service" and noted that
President Eliot, and Dr. Lawrence, dean of the Episcopal theological
school, were on the platform.[60] After adjustments in seating
procedures, *The Crimson* acknowledged: "We are pleased to see
that an opportunity of hearing Professor Drummond in Appleton
Chapel tomorrow will be given exclusively to officers of the
University and their families and to the students. It is expressly
stated that the service will not be open to the public, and we sincerely
hope that this restriction will prevent a repetition of last Sunday's
experience."[61] Even *The Cambridge Tribune* took note: "Professor
Henry Drummond has become a general favorite with Harvard
students. His sincere, straightforward and masterly way of talking
is gaining for him a reputation seldom bestowed on visitors here.
His Sunday evening discourse was attended by one of the largest
audiences that ever assembled in Appleton Chapel."[62] And

[58] *The Daily Crimson*, April 15, 1893.
[59] *The Daily Crimson*, April 16, 1893.
[60] *The Boston Herald*, April 17, 1893.
[61] *The Daily Crimson*, April 22, 1893.
[62] *The Cambridge Tribune*, April 22, 1893.

separation of town from gown did not lessen the crowd: "The public was not invited to Appleton Chapel, Sunday evening, in consequence of the great desire among members of the University to hear Professor Henry Drummond, a proceeding probably without a parallel. Even with this limitation, the chapel was uncomfortably crowded."[63]

Perhaps the opening paragraph of a front page story best sums up Drummond's last visit to Harvard:

> Boylston Hall was filled to overflowing last evening by an audience composed wholly of students. For an hour Professor Drummond held their closest attention; his words were simple, even informal, the thoughts to which he gave expression were familiar, and if spoken by an ordinary man would have seemed trite and commonplace. Yet the strong intellectualism, the broad tolerance, the ready wit, and above all, the sincerity, earnestness, straightforwardness and manliness of the speaker gave to his words a penetrating significance that makes his address one of the most powerful, as it was one of the most remarkable, to which Harvard students have ever listened.[64]

Harvard students could not seem to get enough of Drummond. Invited to tea at Mrs. Agassiz's home one May afternoon, more than two weeks after his last public lecture at Harvard, students pleaded with Drummond to address them yet again, either then or at some future date. "Much to their disappointment," he declined, pleading shyness, and the incident found mention in the local newspaper.[65]

From Harvard it was on to Amherst, where *The Amherst Student* proudly gave notice of Drummond's forthcoming appearance in the College Church, claiming: "Professor Drummond is the author of many well-known religious works and addresses, among which may be mentioned, *Natural Law in the Spiritual World*, *The Greatest Thing in the World*, *Pax Vobiscum*, etc. His influence in the religious world may be said to be second to none. The College may well be

[63] *The Cambridge Tribune*, April 29, 1893.
[64] *The Cambridge Tribune*, April 18, 1893.
[65] *The Cambridge Tribune*, May 6, 1893.

congratulated on securing the privilege of hearing him."[66] Afterward, an *Amherst Student* editorial marked the special event: "Much space in this issue has been devoted to Sunday's sermon, which will long live in the memory of those who heard it. It is seldom the College has the rare opportunity of listening to one, whose life work and character have made such an impression upon the world in general. Of the sermon itself nothing need be said. Its simplicity, interest and conciseness, and the manner in which it was delivered, made it a model of its kind. In Professor Drummond himself, an honorary graduate, and a loyal friend of Amherst, the College has the heartiest interest." "The address was one of the best that has been heard in the College course of sermons. . . ."[67]

From the eastern college / university circuit, Drummond made his way to the great World's Columbian Exposition in Chicago, where he rendezvoused with the Aberdeens. Lady Aberdeen was leading patron and president of the Irish Industrial Association Village, an effort to promote cottage industries of lace-making and sewing to help the working classes, and which had a demonstration and sales pavilion at the Exposition. The Aberdeens were there to herald its opening, managing even to get their cause before President Grover Cleveland. Drummond went on to Minneapolis and Duluth, and back to Chautauqua and Northfield for Moody's summer conference. He then made his way to Canada to meet his friend, W. E. Dodge, his host at a posh private fishing resort. Drummond wrote his mother on the stationery of the Restigouche Salmon Club, Metapedia, Quebec, July 15, 1893, that they were enjoying a houseboat pulled along the river by horses, and sometimes staying in clubhouses along the way, fishing as they went. He noted that the average salmon caught by club members the previous year was $26\frac{1}{2}$ pounds.[68]

When he saw Lord and Lady Aberdeen in Chicago, he must have realized how close geographically they would be later on,

---

[66] *The Amherst Student*, May 13, 1893.
[67] *The Amherst Student*, May 20, 1893.
[68] Smith, Drummond, pp. 417–425.

and he must have promised to meet the Aberdeens when they officially arrived to be installed as Governor-General of Canada. In *We Twa*, the memoirs of the Aberdeens, it is noted that "Henry Drummond was there, too, true to his promise . . ." and his devotional on the 46th Psalm was part of their Sunday evening service that first evening in the Ballroom of the Governor-General's residence.[69] August and September having been dedicated to rest and relaxation in Canada, he returned to Chicago in early October to speak at the opening convocation of the University of Chicago's second year, and to address the Evangelical Alliance of the United States which that year (October 8–14, 1893) took the form of an International Christian Conference. He thought the audiences at the conference especially cordial, and as soon as the conference ended, he left for Glasgow to begin the new academic year.

He would never return to the United States. J. Y. Simpson notes that "When he returned from America, his friends noticed a marked change in his appearance: for the first time it was apparent that he was growing old."[70] Gradually, he began to show signs of weakness, and could be taken sharply ill, apparently dealing with the symptoms of the affliction that would gradually claim his life in March of 1897 – perhaps bone cancer.

To evaluate Henry Drummond's contribution from this perspective, one hundred years after his death, it seems appropriate to observe:

1. Few men in modern Christian history have so consistently enjoyed such total admiration from their close friends, and so consistently been evaluated as among the most Christlike. Even among friends, personal envy can be strong, a sense of competition sometimes asserts itself, and honesty ultimately breaks through. But unlike even many greater figures of church history, there seem to be few chinks in the armor of Christlikeness claimed for Drummond by his close friends.

[69] Lord and Lady Aberdeen, *We Twa*, Vol. I, pp. 13–14.
[70] Simpson, *Drummond*, p. 94.

2. At a time when the church and Christian community were struggling with science and seeing science as foe, Drummond approached science unafraid and urged others to do so. He saw science as further revelation of God and, thus, a friend to organized religion. While he may have been a bit overeager to embrace the claims of science – for religion to accommodate science or for science to make way for religion – he pointed evangelical Christianity toward awareness and acceptance of science.

3. After World War II, ministries specific to college / university students became commonplace in both Britain and the United States. But Drummond was among the earliest expressly to focus on capturing the hearts and minds of future leadership by ministering to the upcoming generation in the formative years of university life. His biographer, G. A. Smith, wrote Drummond's mother from Cleveland, Ohio where he was lecturing at the time, a letter dated May 22, without a year specified, but most likely 1901.

> I have found I have not overestimated his work among students. I have rather underestimated it. I have been among many colleges in this country and have been surprised with the readiness of the students to hear the religious, and with the strength of religion, and with the strength and wisdom with which the university YMCA's are being conducted. In Yale, I had five meetings with the men on a Sunday evening and following days – from 300 to 500 were always present. Religion has nowhere in America such promise for the future as among students. Well, the whole thing, under God, is due to Henry and especially to his first visit to the American colleges. My pride in him has been steadily rising. Everywhere, the still, strong, and, I trust, growing involvement found its initiative in his addresses and personal influence.[71]

4. It is uncommon that persons on the intellectual frontiers are deeply concerned about evangelism – yet that combination was ever-present in Drummond. And, to be sure, his was never a superficial, transactional telling of the Good News. His was a reasonable, courteous, reflective, life-style evangelism.

[71] Letter, G. A. Smith to Mrs. Drummond, May 22, 1901. Drummond Papers.

5. Over and again, virtuous words like "sincerity," "simplicity," "straightforwardness" seem to characterize Henry Drummond's speaking, his witness, his *persona*.

Not in the one hundred years since his death has Britain sent to America a Christian ambassador of the popular stature of Henry Drummond. If we learn by example, may the significance of his life and work instruct us even now.

6

❦

Response

Robin S. Barbour

First of all, I would like to say a very big thank you on my own behalf, especially, but also on Richard Buckley's, no doubt, to you, not only for inviting us here and treating us so very generously and letting us see this lovely place, but also for continuing an interest which to our shame in Scotland, we have really abandoned – the interest in an important figure in the history of the church, and indeed, in some ways in Western society, Henry Drummond. So, I am very grateful for that, and I am also personally grateful in this way, that it so happens that both on my father's and my mother's sides of the family, we have close connections. My grandfather, whose name I bear, and Henry Drummond were very close, personal friends. I was brought up to some extent in the knowledge of that fact. My mother was a great-niece of John Marquess of Aberdeen, and so there was a connection there, too. I personally am very delighted that here in Samford University, we remember this great man. That one marvelously successful bust, which our friend, Glynn Acree, has produced, will I am sure keep him in the minds of many of us here.

Let me just make one or two very brief comments, if I may, on what has been so admirably said by President and Mrs. Corts about Drummond and Drummond in America. There are so many things that they said that are important. The man lives for us all now, I think, in a way in which he didn't before. Could I just add one or two little things that have occurred to me from my particular

91

background as matters which might help us to understand him and to assess his significance?

First of all, on science and religion, I think it is true that Drummond is partly forgotten today because his great contribution – and it was a great contribution to the whole science and religion debate at the end of the last century – is not really relevant any longer. But, I would like to say one thing about it because it seems to me that this general principle may indeed still be relevant. His first very popular and major work, a book of over 400 pages, *Natural Law in the Spiritual World,* was arguing that there were indeed two worlds: the world of science, investigated by natural law; and the world of the human spirit. The thing which made him original, as I understand the matter, was that he was prepared to argue that these two worlds were really one world in this way: In both of these worlds, the Lord God, who is consistent, operates in accordance with certain laws which are in accordance with His will. This applies, Drummond said, to the spiritual world as much as it did to the natural laws of the scientific world. This rang a very loud bell, if you like, made a very strong impression on the generation of Henry Drummond's time. It is hard, I think, for us to gauge just what a bad way the church was in that respect after Charles Darwin and Lamarck and the rest of them had started to make clear the evolutionary understanding of the world that science represented. I will not try to say more than that at the moment, but I think this was very important because you see it was an attempt to assert one world again and that appealed to very many people.

Today, new charges, *mutatis mutandi* something of the same sort, I think, might be said. The later big book, *The Ascent of Man*, the Lowell Lectures is a book which shows Drummond's fundamental optimistic faith. Not faith in human nature really, but faith in God. Because he was an optimist, as Charles Darwin most certainly wasn't, he was an optimist because he believed in the living Lord, and that you see, also appealed to people enormously. It wasn't just the personal faith that he emphasizes in his evangelical work, which itself was supremely important, but he was signaling the possibility of believing in God in a new and broader way.

And if I might make just a quick comment to that point, it seems to me that his background is significant, and his friendships are significant, too. I said that the church, I thought, in later-Victorian times in relation to Darwinism and so on was, as a matter of fact, in a surprisingly bad way, although that wasn't very evident to many people. That doesn't mean to say that there wasn't considerable activity, of course, in the church. In Scotland in the nineteenth century when Drummond was still a little boy, there had been the great 1859 revival which had swept across the eastern parts of the country, not the Gaelic-speaking parts so much – they had another one later – and there was, indeed, a renewed evangelical faith and fervour among a great many people. This is part of Drummond's background. For example, his friend – a great man – Alexander Whyte, Minister of Free St. George's in Edinburgh for many years, was the illegitimate child of a very poor woman in the little weaving town of Coillebhrochain. Whyte's mother had struggled to get him an education and succeeded. Alexander Whyte had been influenced, indeed, by the revivals of the 1859 and 1873, too. He was a slightly older contemporary of Drummond and knew him well. He and others like him were on the one hand very powerfully affected by this evangelical revival in Scotland, but on the other hand, were also powerfully affected by the close Scottish links with Germany. This is very important, I think, in the background of Henry Drummond and others. The Scots had discovered the Germans' scholarship, and after being a little bit frightened of it to begin with, many of them had accepted it wholeheartedly. It was at that source that many people, like George Adam Smith and others – including my grandfather – drank. They went to Tübingen and Göttingen, and they imbibed this. What came out at the end of this was a kind of broad evangelicalism, which was not fundamentalist at all, but which accepted most of, not all, of course, but most of what was being said about biblical criticism, seeing it as something constructive and not something destructive and again because of the kind of faith in one world, one God, which Drummond evinced in relation to science. This is an important part of his background.

So, we find Drummond loved the word "broad," it tended to become a good word for him, a praise word; whereas, "narrow" tended to be a word of criticism. So, there is a broad and tolerant evangelicalism, which is a very powerful spiritual force in the circles in which Drummond grew up. But that is not to say that he wasn't himself a very distinctive character. President Corts has said quite a lot about the remarkable way in which he influenced individuals, and that is something which I really wouldn't like to try to comment on further. But, it was certainly there.

One of the interesting things about Drummond is that he is in the real sense the first *student* pastor. There weren't any in the Western world; there weren't any, I don't think, in the States; there certainly weren't any in Europe, until the end of the last century. It is interesting to me that in my grandparents' house, Bronskeid, Perthshire, in 1889 and 1890, there were held two meetings of University men (they were called; they were all men in those days), initiated and stimulated by Henry Drummond. And what were they? They were the beginnings, in fact, of the Student Christian Movement and of Christian Unions and other work of that kind all over the world. I like to think in my self-centered, Scot-centered way that it was rather marvelous that in my grandparents' home, something started that has spread all around the world.

Now, President Corts said quite rightly – gave a theological explanation of the remarkable gifts evinced and seen in men like Henry Drummond, George Adam Smith, Alexander Whyte, and others. His theological explanation, which is entirely correct – can I say such a thing about a University President, that he has a correct opinion? Yes, I think so.

Scotland's need was so desperate that the good Lord poured out His grace upon these people and saved us from total oblivion, if not total depravity. I have another explanation, too, and that is, that the good Lord brought together a lot of different strands in a kind of way that produced this very remarkable mixture and this very remarkable result. That is a theological explanation, too. You know, we are all the victims of original sin, and one of the things about that is that the Scots like hearing themselves decried. That is why we want a little more independence! But, I am not going to introduce irrelevancies. I want simply to say, thank you very much for welcoming us, and thank you for preserving the memory of this great man.

7

"The greatest thing in the world" – Henry Drummond on love

Robin S. Barbour

My song is love unknown;
My Saviour's love to me.
Love to the loveless shown,
That they might lovely be.
O who am I,
That for my sake
My Lord should take
Frail flesh, and die.[1]

I mention that hymn of Samuel Crossman's, written in England rather more than three hundred years ago, because its seven verses are as good an example as I know of the story of Jesus' life and death told by one who sees it also as the story of the love of God for us all, given freely and once for all. Paul, too, has a story to tell, the story of the love of God for us all, given freely and once for all. He tells it in a number of places and a number of ways, and

---

[1] Samuel Crossman, "My Song is Love Unknown," in *The Young Man's Meditation, or some Few Sacred Poems upon Select Subjects, and Scriptures* (London, 1664), pp. 8–10. Later published with music as "Love Unknown," by Daniel Sedgwick (London, 1863) and in the *Anglican Hymn Book* (London, 1868).

nowhere more movingly than in the words which we have just heard read to us. But, am I justified in saying that this is the story of the love of God for us all in Jesus Christ? Neither God nor Jesus is mentioned in this famous hymn about love. It would be possible, I suppose, to give an interpretation of it in which its specifically Christ-centered meaning is played down or even ignored. Indeed the great German scholar Werner Jaeger did once argue that the model for it is to be found in earlier Greek writings about virtue; the great Christian virtue is love, and this is a hymn of the Christians patterned on Greek antecedents.

I want to suggest that this is wrong; that Paul has God and His love for us in Christ quite as much in mind here as anywhere, and that his model, if he had one, for the shape of the chapter was not a Greek one. But, I draw attention to this question because I think that to consider it may help us to understand what Henry Drummond was doing when he wrote his marvelous piece about *The Greatest Thing in the World*. We are met to honour Drummond and to thank God for his work here in America, of which *The Greatest Thing in the World* was an important part.

I am sure you are all aware that it is not easy to tell from a study of Paul's letters how much he knew of what we now find told to us about Jesus in the Gospels. He quotes words and actions of *Jesus* just occasionally – most importantly with regard to the Last Supper – but although many scholars have found echoes of words of Jesus in Paul's letters, direct quotations are very few. It can't be my business here to go into this matter in any detail, but I do want to ask a question about I Corinthians 13 in this connection. How did Paul come to the marvelously deep and rich understanding of love which he shows here? He is, of course, using the Greek word for one kind of love – *agape* – which the translators of the Old Testament into Greek used when they wanted a word for God's love for His people, and which, therefore, became the special word for that love in the New Testament, too. Paul is not just talking about love as anyone might do; he must be talking about God's love, and he must be talking about that love poured out on his people as a gift of his Spirit, his whole argument is concern to show that love is the greatest of all God's gifts to his people, and it is a personal argument against his Corinthian converts who seemed to think otherwise. Drummond does not explicitly mention this in his great address – it was not his primary concern; but neither does he raise another question which is interesting and important for us today. How far does Paul's picture of love depend on what he actually knew of Jesus and his example, his words and his deeds, his life and his death? And how far does it come from some other source? When he says: "Love is patient; love is kind; love is not envious or boastful or arrogant or rude. It does not insist on its own way; it is not irritable or resentful; it does not rejoice in wrongdoing, but rejoices in the truth" (I Corinthians 13:4–6). When he says that, he does not appear to be following known models, Greek or otherwise. Is he then copying what he sees in the stories about Jesus, if he knew them? Henry Drummond of course, like Samuel Crossman before him, knew his Gospels and undoubtedly could and did follow them: but with Paul it is not so easy to be sure.

What I want to suggest to you, quite tentatively, is that Paul is here following the example of Christ, but not so much because he knew a lot of stories about Jesus which could lead to the memorable picture of love in action that he paints, rather because, ever since the vision on the Damascus road, the Risen Lord had been with him and influenced him, had poured out his Spirit upon him, in such a profoundly moral or ethical, and of course, spiritual way, that he had a vision of what Jesus' pilgrimage in life must have been, a vision which enabled him to speak of God's Spirit, who is also Jesus' Spirit, in the intensely moving way in which he does. In this respect Paul seems different from many others who followed him after the Gospels were written, like Samuel Crossman whom I quoted; but the striking thing, and I want to come back to this, is that what we come to in the end is so much the same.

But if there is any truth at all in that conjecture about Paul, there is another thing that has to be added, a feature of I Corinthians 13 that also separates it from any Greek parallels. This is that it is all about the new life in the Kingdom towards which Paul believed he and all God's people were being rapidly driven forward. In the new world of the Kingdom many things will come to an end, but not love. And that distinguishes it from most of the other gifts that many Christians would love to have: prophecy, special knowledge of different kinds, heroic self-sacrifice, and much more. Paul is being driven to emphasize the greatness of love even more than he would otherwise do because this is the nature of God's victory in the future as it was in the past. The sign of the Cross will be in the heavens when the Lord comes to reign.

Drummond knows this, but it is perhaps not surprising that he does not greatly emphasize it. He is concerned with what is the greatest thing in the world now. And while he has the figure of Christ in his mind always, most of what he actually says comes from observation of people. Let us take one example only. "Love," says Paul, "is not irritable" (I Corinthians 13:5, New Revised Standard), as one modern translation puts it; "is never quick to take offense" (I Corinthians 13:5, New English), says another; "is not easily angered" (I Corinthians 13:5, NIV) says another (rather less happily, I think); "is not easily provoked" (I Corinthians 13:5) says the King James version (why did anyone ever bother to change that?). Drummond calls this aspect of love "good temper,"[2] and here is part of what he says about it:

> Love is not easily provoked. Nothing could be more striking than to find this here. We are inclined to look upon bad temper as a very harmless weakness. We speak of it as a mere infirmity of nature, a family failing, a matter of temperament, not a thing to take into very serious account in estimating a man's character. And yet here, right in the heart of this analysis of love, it finds a place. . . .
>
> The peculiarity of ill temper is that it is the vice of the virtuous. It is often the one blot on an otherwise noble character. You know men who are all but perfect, and women who would be entirely perfect, but for an easily ruffled, quick-tempered or "touchy" disposition. This compatibility of ill temper with high moral character is one of the strangest and saddest problems of ethics. . . . No form of vice, not worldliness, not greed of gold, not drunkenness itself, does more to unChristianize society than evil temper. For embittering life, for breaking up communities, for destroying the

[2] Drummond, *The Greatest Thing*.

most sacred relationships, for devastating homes, for withering up men and women, for taking the bloom off childhood, in short, for sheer gratuitous misery-producing power, this influence stands alone.[3]

Drummond goes on to illustrate what he is saying from the figure of the elder brother in the so-called parable of the prodigal son. All this is strong stuff; the man is a great rhetorician, whatever else he is. But the point I want to stress is this.

Drummond goes on to say that to get rid of ill temper, "We must go to the source, and change the inmost nature, and the angry humors will die away of themselves. Souls are made sweet not by taking the acid fluids out, but by putting something in – a great Love, a new Spirit, the Spirit of Christ."[4] That is really the center of his contention, as it is of Paul's. This great Love, this new Spirit, the Spirit of Christ, must inform and penetrate the virtuous just as much as the vicious. The commands of virtue, indeed the commands of God, must themselves be obeyed in love and in no other way. Love, as Paul says elsewhere, is the fulfilling of the law. It is better, as Drummond goes on to say, not to live than not to love.

But that is just what seems utterly impossible to many a sincere person. How can I love to order? I may seek to honor my father and mother, but if they do not love me – and in some cases they do not – how can I love them in return? I may be able to keep others of the commandments, like not committing adultery, but when Jesus pushes me further and tells me I must never look on a woman to lust after her, how can I love her when I'm busy trying not to do just that? At this point, no doubt, someone will cry out for some sort of analysis of different kinds of love; and there is not time for that here. But in a way it does not matter; for what we're thinking about and what I'm trying to talk about is that something that is not within our capacity to produce but only within our capacity to receive. It is, to quote Paul yet again, "the grace of our Lord Jesus Christ, and the love of God, and the

[3] Drummond, *The Greatest Thing.*
[4] Ibid.

common sharing in the Holy Spirit" (II Corinthians 13:13) that we are thinking about; and as my beloved teacher Donald Baillie taught me with great clarity many years ago, there is a paradox about this grace of the Lord Jesus Christ, this free gift from Him. It is that the more we recognize it to be a gift from Him, and a gift of the very love of God Himself, the more we are able to see it also as our own possession, that which flows into and out of us and for which therefore we are in the fullest sense ourselves responsible. It is the only thing that makes a common life worth living in the fullest sense; and it is best called love.

Now it is worth noticing very briefly how these two such different men, St. Paul and Henry Drummond, build their thoughts into a whole. Both are quite plainly speaking of love as a human quality, and speaking of it as a result of their experience of life; to go no further, Paul is speaking of so-called gifts of the Spirit and their effect in the life of early Christian congregations, and Drummond is speaking of what he has seen in the societies of northern Europe and America just over a hundred years ago. Both men have the gift of seeing these things with the eye of an acute observer and with the insight given by the power of Christ. Both – not just the observer's eye but also the gift of the powerful insight from the Christ they know – both together form the Spirit's gift and make it possible to discern the love of God in human realities. The only satisfactory analysis of what is happening is thus a Trinitarian one, and it is important to see that what I have called the eye of an acute observer is part of the gift of the Spirit; and it is something that is inevitably related to the changing situations and forms in which human life expresses itself. What Paul expressed in one form in the first century we shall necessarily seek to express in another; so that the Bible itself can never be taken as a straight guide to twentieth-century life – though many think it can. But a truly Trinitarian account of what God has done, is doing and will do with his people, within which the Bible has an important, and indeed a unique place, that indeed can bring us light and truth for our day.

So in 1997, as we look back with gratitude to God for what was achieved by his servant Henry Drummond a hundred years ago and more, we must look at his work again with as much historical precision as we can muster, and above all with a Trinitarian understanding of what God the Father, God the Son, and God the Holy Spirit was doing in him. It is a remarkable fact that his piece on I Corinthians 13, *The Greatest Thing in the World*, has been in print ever since it was published at the beginning of 1874. We can benefit from it still; we can enjoy its style, its conciseness in a world of prolix speech, its impact upon us in other ways, too. Listen to him again,

> Where love is, God is. He that dwelleth in love dwelleth in God. God is love. Therefore, *love*, without distinction, without calculation, without procrastination, love. Lavish it upon the poor, where it is very easy; especially upon the rich, who often need it most; most of all upon our equals, where it is very difficult, and for whom perhaps we each do least of all.[5]

What about those words? Will they stand today? We cannot forget that when Drummond spoke and wrote, no one had heard much of Marx and no one had heard of Freud. Today, we have learnt that a command to love which does not take justice into account, and a command to love individuals which takes no account of necessary changes in society, is not likely to be God's word for us.

Today, we have learnt that any account of human motivation which ignores subconscious aims and influences is not likely to be God's word for us. Yes, but today we have also learnt that, in the light of what Marx and Freud and many others have taught us in the days since Drummond spoke, there can be a much deeper understanding of how the Holy Spirit works in the complex psyche of the human being and in the complexities of human society than there ever was before. For, as I tried to say, the Spirit does not come as an alien force into human situations, but, since it, or he, or she, is the Spirit of the incarnate Christ, the Spirit comes within the totality of every human situation and rescues it from lovelessness and degradation.

[5] Drummond, *The Greatest Thing*.

And it is still as true today as it was when Paul spoke, when Samuel Crossman sang, and when Drummond poured out his eloquence before fascinated masses in university and college and hall – it is still as true today as it was then that in a world where everything withers and dies, love – God's love in Christ – does not. Love never fails. For that, we give thanks to God today. And for the way in which Henry Drummond proclaimed it in America to our great-grandfathers, and indeed proclaims it still to us, we give thanks to him too. *Soli Deo Gloria. Amen.*

Appendices

Appendix A

❧

First Corinthians 13

C. K. O. Spence

*Presented to the congregation
of the Henry Drummond Parish Church of Scotland,
98 Allander Street, Glasgow, Scotland, Sunday, February 2, 1958,
in the 70th Anniversary Year of publication of*
The Greatest Thing in the World.

The theme of our service this morning is Paul's magnificent 13th chapter of First Corinthians. Few passages of Scripture have inspired so much compelling and enduring devotional writings as this chapter. Perhaps, the best known and loved of all is the little book by Henry Drummond which he entitled *The Greatest Thing in the World*. Published first in 1888, it is a best-seller still today, seventy years later. We who form the congregation of the church which Henry Drummond founded in 1881 invite you to join with us in giving thanks to God for the life and enduring witness of a great evangelist.

Prayer

Almighty God, our Heavenly Father, before whom all the world is as one family, we gather in Thy presence in humble prayer and supplication. The word of Him who of old walked beside the troubled ways of human sin and sorrow has called us unto Thee, to lay before Thee now our needs in prayer.

We need Thee every day, for the increasing burden of the world lies heavy upon us. We grow weary of the daily task and our lack of

107

faith hinders us in the way of duty and of service. Our sins increase the sorrow of our separation from Thee; and without Thee there is no light anywhere.

We confess that we have chosen ways that are dark and set with thorns. We have followed selfish and foolish desires. We are at war with ourselves. Our best would rise to Thee, but our worst would keep us in the darkness and the dust. By our self-will, envy, and pride we have added to the bitterness and sadness of mankind.

When we remember, our hearts are heavy within us, and we yearn to behold Thy love revealed in Christ – His perfect purity, His eternal peace, His charity that never faltered, His sympathy that never failed in a world of selfishness and pain.

Father of all Mercy, help us to seek Thy pardon as we ought. Make us worthy of Christ's sacrifice. Help us to the great surrender of all we have and all we are in the service of our fellows for His sake. Help us to take up our Cross daily, to deny ourselves, and to acknowledge Him as our Lord and Master.

Hear Thou our prayers, O, God; and grant us an answer in Thy mercy; for Jesus' sake. Amen.

Scripture Lesson

Let us hear the Word of God as it is contained in the First Epistle of Paul to the Corinthians, Chapter 13, and at the first verse.

Though I speak with the tongues of men and of angels, and have not love, I am become as sounding brass, or a tinkling cymbal. And though I have the gift of prophecy, and understand all mysteries, and all knowledge; and though I have all faith, so that I could remove mountains, and have not love, I am nothing. And though I bestow all my goods to feed the poor, and though I give my body to be burned, and have not love, it profiteth me nothing.

Love suffereth long, and is kind; love envieth not; love vaunteth not itself, is not puffed up. Doth not behave itself unseemly, seeketh not her own, is not easily provoked, thinketh no evil; rejoiceth not in iniquity, but rejoiceth in the truth; beareth all things, believeth all things, hopeth all things, endureth all things. Love never faileth . . .

And now abideth faith, hope, love, these three; but the greatest of these is love. (I Corinthians 13:1–13, New American Standard)

Sermon

Love is the greatest thing in the world. That is triumphant and confident claim of Paul. The Apostle John goes even further when he wrote: God *is* love. and that is the last word on faith; the sum total of all belief. That is what Christ came to tell the world; that was the message of His life and example. Love was the reason why He died upon a cross, and love the power by which He rose again. His one commandment to His disciples was love God and one another. Love from beginning to end, and, claims Paul, it never fails.

But is love the greatest thing in the world? The whole evidence of history supports the claim. Every age has had its heroes of faith; men and women who loved freedom and truth more than their own lives. Even our own sad and divided world has faith and determination enough to go on seeking for a lasting peace, which is the fairest of the fruits of love. The unity of every nation is built upon love and loyalty to a common purpose, and a common trust. The very pattern of human life is founded upon the love of a man and a woman who bring forth their child in love. The infant's cry stilled by the embrace of a mother's arms, is the symbol of a world which from cradle to grave, yearns for and is reassured and nurtured by, the understanding, acceptance, trust and companionship of love. If any doubt should remain that love *is* the greatest thing in the world, then ask yourself the question: what happens when nations stop striving for peace, doctors stop healing the sick, men cease caring for the hungry, and distressed? No doubt about the answer, and it settles the issue once and for all. If these things should ever happen, it is the end of hope, of life itself. Yes indeed, Paul's claim is vindicated.

Perhaps you may feel, in the light of such a claim, that love has not made a very great success of our world. Love still has a lot of work to do. Love works slowly, but whenever it has been honestly and sincerely tried, it has never failed. And love is still working its miracles today. For example, think of this. Yesterday, Christians were glorying in their divisions, but today they know that disunity is a sin. True they are sore perplexed to know how to resolve it, but the miracle of love has brought us to that awareness, and I am persuaded that the miracle of love will one day make us all one in Christ.

But all this must start with you and me if it is to start anywhere. Christ is pleading with us through the pages of His Word and through the working of the Holy Spirit to take Him at His Word; to get behind our theology and our ecclesiasticism to the divine simplicity which is the hallmark of authentic faith. That divine simplicity states the irrefutable – on Calvary love triumphed. It triumphs still. To be a Christian is to possess in some measure the Spirit of Christ, and love is the contribution we can all make, even the meekest and humblest. O restless soul whoever you are, find your rest in Him who came to seek and to save that which was lost! Know the peace of His forgiveness, the comfort of His presence! And then go forth and use His love to save His world. You who are seeking for a meaning and purpose to your life, you will find it here.

Lastly, a glorious yet sobering thought. Not only the past and the present belong to love, but the future also. Glorious, because God is Love, and love is the guarantee that hate and fear, and falsehood, all enmity and bitterness, are doomed. The victory belongs to the love that was crucified and rose again. A sober thought as well, because by that same love we shall one day be judged. I leave with you the words with which Henry Drummond closes his book, *The Greatest Thing in the World,* as fresh and compelling today as they were seventy years ago when they were written.

> It is the Son of MAN before whom the nations of the world shall be gathered. It is in the presence of HUMANITY that we shall be charged. And the spectacle of it will silently judge each one. Those will be there whom we have met and helped; or there, the unpitied multitude whom we neglected or desired. No other Witness need be summoned. No other charge than lovelessness shall be preferred. Be not deceived. The words which all of us shall one day hear, sound

not of theology but of life, not of churches and saints but of the hungry and of the poor, not of creeds and doctrines but of shelter and of clothing, not of Bibles and prayer-books but of cups of cold water in the name of Christ. Thank God that the Christianity of today is coming nearer the world's need. Live to help that on. Thank God men know better, by a hairsbreadth, what religion is, what God is, who Christ is, where Christ is. Who is Christ? He who fed the hungry, clothed the naked, visited the sick. And where is Christ? Where? – who so shall receive a little child in My name receiveth Me. And who are Christ's? Everyone that loveth is born of God.

In Christ's Name, I urge you to give love a chance in your life today, and to God be the glory.

Prayer and Lord's Prayer

Let us pray.

O God, whose Providence is ever watchful over all that Thou hast made, and whose love is as near as the beating of our own hearts, in Thy mercy accept our prayers for all humanity. Blessing Thee for Thy gifts to us, of human love and friendship, and for Thy love in Jesus Christ our Lord, we would bring to Thee in the fellowship of our prayers, all whom Thou hast made dear to us – all who are with us in the unity of the faith – all who are seeking Thy help and consolation in life's common need and sorrow, the toiling, the suffering, the sick, the lonely and the dying. Give unto them, O Lord, the same blessing which we ask for ourselves. Remember the poor and the naked, the hungry and the thirsty, the wandering and the lost, the friendless and the despairing.

We pray for Thy Son's Church. Open the way for the preaching of Thy Gospel everywhere; and hasten the time when all the world shall be truly Thine. Unite and strengthen the Church of Christ in all the world; and keep the cross free from the stain and shadow of human pride. Bless all who love Thee and seek to serve Thee; and give Thy strength and support to every heart that would bring men nearer Thee.

We pray for the nations of the world. Kindle in the hearts of all men the true love of peace, and guide with Thy pure and peaceable wisdom those who at this time take counsel for the nations of the earth; that in tranquility Thy kingdom may go forward, till the earth be filled with the knowledge of Thy love.

These our prayers we offer in Jesus' Name who taught us when we pray to say:

Our Father which art in heaven, Hallowed be Thy Name. Thy kingdom come. Thy will be done in earth, as it is in heaven. Give us this day our daily bread. And forgive us our debts, as we forgive our debtors. And lead us not into temptation, but deliver us from evil: For thine is the kingdom, and the power, and the glory, for ever. Amen. (Matthew 6:9-13, King James)

Appendix B

❦

A note about
The Greatest Thing in the World

In any age, it is difficult to predict how successfully a book will
sell, but apparently, a number of Drummond's contemporaries
never considered that *The Greatest Thing in the World* (*TGTITW*)
would be his best-seller. At the time, his fame seemed to be based
more upon *Natural Law in the Spiritual World* and *The Ascent of
Man*, both now long out-of-print and considered anachronisms.
John Watson remarked in his essay of tribute that ". . . his tract on
'Charity' will long be read . . ." (*The Ideal Life*, p. 41). And Cuthbert
Lennox, whose book was originally published in 1901, commented
upon *The Greatest Thing*'s "unprecedented" sale (p. 147). But the
book's success is not discussed in George Adam Smith's biography
and, though other Drummond titles appear in the indexes,
TGTITW does not rate a place in the index of either the Smith or
Simpson volumes.

Confusion, both then and now, surrounds the early publication
of *TGTITW*. Evidence indicates that the essay had been presented
orally by Henry Drummond many times, perhaps over ten or fifteen
years, prior to publication. It first came to the attention of evangelist
D. L. Moody in 1884, and it was he who was most insistent that
the essay be published, though Moody had heard it only once as a
devotional talk.

It appears to have been duplicated in some form prior to
authorized publication, perhaps reduced from inaccurate transcripts
and without Drummond's review, editing, or consent. In an article
that appeared in *The Christian Herald*, March 25, 1897, following
his death, a journalist recalled this story told to him by Henry
Drummond.

The Americans have made me shy of journalists. In whatever strict privacy I might think I was delivering an address, it would shortly be reported – and alas! reported in a way that made it altogether unrecognizable to me – the next day. It was like this with "The Greatest Thing in the World." I had given the address at a small quiet meeting, never thinking any more about it. After a while, at a Swiss hotel, a booklet was handed to me by a lady across the dinner table, and, lo and behold, it was my address. I had not intended it for publication, so, in self-defense, I revised it.

The first Drummond-authorized printing of the address came in 1887. Drummond gave the message at Moody's summer student conference at Northfield (Massachusetts) and the proceedings of the conference were published in a volume, *A College of Colleges: Led by D. L. Moody*, published in 1887 by Moody's brother-in-law who ran the Fleming H. Revell publishing enterprise. That volume includes transcripts of conversations and talks given by Drummond in a question-and-answer setting, in addition to the complete text of *Love, the Supreme Gift*, as it was originally titled. That version has a few minor differences from the later published text.

The present writer has a vellum-bound copy of a booklet entitled, *Love – the Supreme Gift: The Greatest Thing in the World*, published by Fleming H. Revell, and bearing the copyright date "1887–90." It appears to be word-for-word, exactly as the transcription in *A College of Colleges* (1887), which would indicate that it is one of the older versions. Almost all 1890-dated editions have a last paragraph that is slightly different from earlier versions.

Lennox's biography (p. 147) states that *TGTITW* was issued at Christmas, 1889. James W. Kennedy, writing in 1953, cited 1889 as the issue date for *TGTITW* as a separate publication. George Adam Smith's biography does not state a specific date for publication of *TGTITW*, but quotes a letter in the Drummond papers in the National Library of Scotland, tending to confirm that the address had been printed first in 1889. The letter is dated January 17, with no year, but Smith treats it as though written in 1890, and on the original letter someone has penciled "1890." The letter from Drummond to a friend states:

At Christmas-time I tried everywhere, both in Edinburgh and Glasgow, for a bound copy of *Greatest Thing*, but it was nowhere to be found, and no copies are yet forthcoming. On New Year's Day I ordered the fifty thousand from the printers, but the binders cannot get the bound one touched until orders for the other one are executed. However, I hope it will come in a day or two, and I shall then obey your behest, though much against the grain. (Smith, p. 292)

Note the letter states that "the binders cannot get the bound one touched until orders for the other one are executed." Such a statement implies at least three important points: (1) an "other one" would seem to be an unbound edition, which must have been available and, not being bound, perhaps it was only stapled or "stitched," as printers say. (2) Since he was ordering so large a quantity as 50,000, Drummond must have had some sense of the public's interest. No one, then or now, would order 50,000 copies of a book without having some prior indication of the magnitude of demand. (3) If he placed the order on New Year's Day, 1890, it was not available for Christmas until the twelve months hence.

A review in *The Church Review*, February 14, 1890 stated: "This elegant brochure *[TGTITW]*, now in its fifth edition, has been issued by Mr. Drummond at the request of those who desire the *ipsissima verba* of an address delivered by him, on an occasion not specified, which had found its way into several foreign languages" [brackets mine]. Obviously, it could not have been in its fifth edition by February of 1890, the date of the above letter, unless it had been issued prior to Christmas, 1889.

The present writer is in possession of more than seventy different editions of *Greatest Thing*. One green clothbound copy was issued by Hodder & Stoughton from London with copyright date of 1890, and with a handwritten inscription by the giver of the book, "Xmas 1890." The same copy has printed on the title page its identification as the "SIXTEENTH EDITION" and with the further note: "COMPLETING TWO HUNDRED AND FIFTY THOUSAND." It would have been impossible for the book to have been released just a few weeks, and already to have sold sixteen editions and 250,000 copies.

In another letter from the Drummond papers in the National Library of Scotland, dated "Autumn, 1890," Drummond writes his mother about his having bought at auction a silver tea set and some Wedgwood dinnerware. He explains that "They come from 'The Greatest Thing's' pennies." If he had amassed enough "pennies" from *TGTITW* by autumn of 1890, to equal 10 or 15 pounds, the book would have had to have been in print quite some months. Therefore, it could not have been first printed at Christmastime, 1890.

Also in the Drummond papers collection is a letter from Henry Drummond to a printer, dated "16 March 1889," and stating:

> Dear Sir: Would you kindly print other *five thousand* copies of booklet "The Greatest Thing in the World" and forward to Messrs. Hodder & Stoughton. To remain Yours sincerely, Henry Drummond

Yet another letter in the same collection at the National Library of Scotland reads:

> Oct. 16, '89
>
> Booklet– "The Greatest Thing In World"
>
> Dear Sirs:
> The proof is now finally correct with the exception of two corrections. . . . Of course it is quite unnecessary to send further proofs and the printing off may be begun whenever you choose. You might kindly print 5,000 to begin with and keep up type for a little as more will probably be required.
> I think the printing is quite perfect.
>
> Yours sincerely,
> Henry Drummond

It appears that Drummond must have approved publication of *TGTITW* as a separate booklet in some form after the Northfield summer conference in the U.S.A. In addition, he must have decided to do a special edition for Christmas, 1889, launching his Christmas booklet series which covered nine years.

Appendix C

༺ஓ༻

Still among "the greatest"

Among classics of modern Christian literature, a unique place is reserved for Henry Drummond's *The Greatest Thing in the World (TGTITW)*, a practical commentary on I Corinthians 13. Originally published unofficially from inaccurate transcriptions, its first authorized printing was in the United States in 1887, and its first appearance as a separate booklet appears to have come in 1889. The little volume has never been out-of-print, thanks to both secular and religious publishers, having sold at least 10 million copies in at least nineteen languages. The message was, perhaps, an overflow of Drummond's own rich spiritual life.

Modern devotional classics are few in number. At first glance, comparable volumes might be Hannah Whitall Smith's *The Christian's Secret of A Happy Life*, which first appeared as a single volume in 1875 (chapters having been serially published in her husband's little paper, *The Christian's Pathway to Power*) and has sold millions of copies. Charles Sheldon's novel, *In His Steps*, was published in 1896, and has sold over 30 million copies in fifteen languages.

What makes Drummond's little essay so distinctive? We can pose some possible answers.

- It is based upon Scripture. Every edition of *TGTITW* begins with a complete quotation of I Corinthians 13. No other mass sale Christian classic is based upon Bible exposition.

- It is brief. Traditionally, classics are book-length, long enough to appear significant, to stir discussion and to bring recommendations and referrals. Most have sufficient bulk or heft in final, published form to seem a worthy and meritorious gift. Yet, in some editions, *TGTITW* requires as few as seventeen pages.

- *The Greatest Thing* carried the endorsement of D. L. Moody, the world's best-known evangelist of his day.

- Within eight years after his book was published, Drummond was dead at age 45. Smith lived 36 years after publication of her best-known book, and Sheldon was alive more than four decades after *In His Steps* was first printed.

- Smith and Sheldon were Americans who could readily appeal to the American book market, even then larger and more voracious than Britain's. Drummond was a Scot, who made three visits to America, but probably only once, in 1893, after publication of *TGTITW*.

- Early editions of Drummond's book bear no copyright, others were pirated from second-rate transcriptions of his oral presentations and so were reproduced without consent, making it difficult to track the accurate number of copies issued. Both Sheldon's and Smith's books appear to bear copyrights from their earliest editions.

- The subject is timeless, non-doctrinal, non-denominational, and of universal appeal. While many have given the little volume as a wedding gift or as an expression of marital good wishes, it is hard to think of a major event in life for which the sentiments of *TGTITW* would be inappropriate.

- The writer's style, with only a few exceptions, is not embedded with the time-bound characteristics of his era.

Early printings of *TGTITW* happened without Drummond's permission. Yet, his graciousness prevailed, even after he found copies circulating and apparently in multiple languages. He wrote: "I had not intended it for publication, so, in self-defense, I revised it. Translations in sixteen different languages have been sent to me, and, since it seems to have done good, I can say nothing against the chance by which it was made public" (*The Christian Herald*, March 25, 1897).

In fact, Henry Drummond had been refining his message on Love over many years. Even preceding the above incident when his message was transcribed and duplicated without his consent, "The Greatest Thing" in some form was likely given in the follow-up meetings of the Moody–Sankey Campaign of 1874. At least one reference notes that Drummond had given his message on Love during his visit to Africa, and he shared it once with his close circle of friends, known as the Gaiety Club.

As a person of distinctive taste, Drummond had definite ideas about how a book should be crafted. In 1889, after his message on I Corinthians 13 had been set in type at his direction, he sat down to review the galley proofs. Unhappy with the appearance and format, he carried the work to another printer and started over. The second attempt became the first authorized book edition. With its author's final editing and instructions in a letter of October 15, 1889, that "the proof is now correct with two exceptions," *The Greatest Thing in the World* entered the book world in advance of the Christmas season, an oversized "Christmas greeting," printed on deckle-edged paper, with gold-gilt top edge, bound in white covers, all to its author's personal taste and direction. When Drummond died in 1897, it had sold over 330,000 copies in nineteen different languages.

As love is an abstraction, unless it is incarnated, the character of an author adds power to a work on such a subject. In Drummond's case, the quiet self-confident Scot had a wonderful gift both for befriending and for being a friend. Moody, a shrewd judge of character and a man well-acquainted with outstanding Christian personalities of his day, said of Henry Drummond: "As you read what he terms the analysis of love, you find that all its ingredients were interwoven into his daily life, making him one of the most lovable men I have ever known."

Having left to us *The Greatest Thing in the World*, the world is still being blessed with a rich inheritance from Henry Drummond.

Appendix D

❧

Three poems for
Henry Drummond

For Henry on His 34th Birthday at Bonskeid. August 17, 1885
by Robert W. Barbour

Over the Athole hills we went
    over the hills I went with thee,
And! See how half of our years are spent,
    sadly thou said'st to me.

Ah, but the better half remains,
    I answered, if they only bring
the highest fruit of human pains,
    some trophy to the King.

For thee could sense a scarce fore read
    A fuller cup than thine today:
may but the future make the past
    is all a friend can pray.

Ay, and we pray it, whosoe'r,
    have heard thee tell of things above
whether on Plymouth sands or where
    the untamed angoni rove.

And I, nor I alone – who creep
    where thou speedest on,
did thee this prayer in memory keep
    to pray for us anon.

Not for another's gift we crave
    to wear another's crown;
only to live the life He gave
    and then to lay it down.

Written by Robert W. Barbour for Henry Drummond on his 34th birthday, celebrated at Bonskeid.
From the Drummond papers, National Library of Scotland.

HENRY DRUMMOND

Verses Grave and Gay
by George Adam Smith

There's not a grove in Bonskeid Woods
    I see not some dear faces shine,
There's not a path I cannot hear
    The footsteps that once beat with mine!

The past is constant summer here,
    To-day the merest line appears
Of shadow whence I gaze across
    The radiance of those blessed years
        In Bonskeid Woods.

O God, Who flood'st our lonelier days
    With all the sunshine of the past,
If in these narrow straits of Time
    The glory be so full and vast,
What shall we find when by Thy hand
    We break to Open Sea at last!

Written by George Adam Smith with Robert Barbour and Henry Drummond in mind, apparently as he finished his biography of Drummond at Coillebhrochain, near Bonskeid. Reproduced in Lilian Adam Smith, *George Adam Smith: A Personal Memoir and Family Chronicle* (London, 1944), p. 79.

We mourn our loss, for thee we cannot mourn
    Who, standing somewhere in the gold day,
    Upon our murky waste of cold and grey
Dost send Hope's sunshine from beyond the bourne,
And pourest light from that unfailing urn
    Of tender, true Remembrance. Friend alway,
    Friend here, friend there, for all who rise and say
"Father! unto our home we would return!"

Inspirer of the hearts that cannot rest
    Till God who made the heart is surely found,
      Be with us still! and in each cup of cheer
      That old or young shall find for comfort here,
    Give foretaste of that heavenly pleasure-ground
Where Love is Life, and Truth is manifest.

Written by H. D. Rawnsley for the dedication of the Henry Drummond Memorial Fountain in West End (Kelvingrove) Park, Glasgow, March 11, 1902.

Appendix E

The mysterious disappearance of Glasgow's Drummond memorial

An appropriate memorial tribute to Henry Drummond was erected in Glasgow, March 11, 1902, arranged and financed by Lord and Lady Aberdeen. Though property of the city, sometime after 1953, the memorial was removed, and today, no one seems to have knowledge of how and when such an important, historical tribute and work of art could have been lost.

The memorial took the form of a large medallion profile of Drummond in bas relief, created by James Pittendrigh Macgillivray, R.S.A., the King's sculptor for Scotland, mounted on a large sandstone column at the entrance to what was then called "West End Park," today, "Kelvingrove Park," Glasgow. A laurel wreath surrounded the profile, and a modest drinking fountain was mounted beneath the medallion, adding functionality to the tribute, and complementing the biblical text Drummond had used, "There is a river, the streams whereof make glad the city of God," which was inscribed beneath the portrait. His name was at the top of the portrait, and his dates, 1851–1897, were inscribed on a bronze plaque on the opposite side of the column. A copy of the same plaque, without the fountain, still stands today in the entrance foyer of the Haddo House Chapel, and one may still be at Trinity College.

A photograph of the memorial is in the dedicatory program among the Drummond papers collection in the National Library of Scotland. A rough outline, evidence of where the memorial *was*, is still visible on the sandstone column standing at the gates to the Kelvingrove Park entrance near the intersection of streets today known as Woodlands Terrace and Park Terrace. Still evident on the column are the holes made by the hardware attaching the bronze to the stone. When originally located, the memorial was significantly placed close to Drummond's home address after 1885, 3 Park Circus, and within sight of the Free Church College (now Trinity College) where he taught.

In addition to Lord and Lady Aberdeen, the dedication was attended by The Lord Provost (Mr. Samuel Chisholm, L.L.D.), by Macgillivray, the sculptor, and many friends of Drummond, including his biographer, George Adam Smith, and wife, and by Bailie Bilsland, who accepted it on behalf of the Parks Committee of the City of Glasgow. An original poem was authored for the occasion by H. D. Rawnsley. Regret was expressed that Mrs. Drummond, Henry's mother, could not attend due to illness.

According to *The Glasgow Herald*, June, 1902, Lady Aberdeen expressed her feeling that "the Parks Department of the Corporation would value the fountain very highly, and preserve it most carefully for the use of fellow citizens." "Her ladyship said she was sure they could entrust the fountain to no better keeping than that of the Lord Provost of Glasgow, Councile Bilsland, and his colleagues."

While our understanding of public health and hygiene have modified customs relating to public drinking fountains, the memorial would appear to have been appropriate, even without water actively flowing. Yet, today, the entire memorial has vanished. Recent contacts at the fine Glasgow Art Museum, which supposedly maintains a catalog of all municipal artworks, yielded no information. Contacts with the City's Parks office and with the Kelvingrove Park office were to no avail.

What became of the memorial is yet a mystery. James W. Kennedy, in his book, *Henry Drummond: An Anthology* (New York: Harper & Brothers), published in 1953, describes the "beautiful drinking fountain" in the West End Park (p. 61). Dr. Kennedy's witness is that the memorial tribute was still intact in 1953. Indeed, the present writer, upon visiting the Trinity Possil–Henry Drummond Church one recent Sunday morning, was advised by an aged member to be sure to see the Henry Drummond memorial fountain in the park.

It appears that sometime after 1953 the bronze tribute was removed – whether by official action or by vandals, apparently no one knows. Less than a hundred years after the Lord Provost expressed the Corporation's appreciation of the gift "in memory of a distinguished citizen" (*British Weekly*, uncertain date, 1902), the memorial is not to be found. While citizens can regret the loss of public recognition of an important Scotsman and a fine work of art, one can only imagine that Drummond would find wry humor in the mystery of his disappearance.

Selected References

ABERDEEN, LORD and LADY. *We Twa: Reminiscences of Lord and Lady Aberdeen.* London: Collins, 1925.

BARBOUR, I. G. *Issues in Science and Religion.* New York: Harper & Row, 1968.

BAXTER, PAUL. "Science and Belief in Scotland, 1805–1868: The Scottish Evangelicals." Ph.D. diss., University of Edinburgh, 1985.

———. "Deism and Development: Disruptive Forces in Scottish Natural Theology." In *Scotland in the Age of Disruption*, edited by Stewart J. Brown and Michael Fry, 106–108. Edinburgh: Edinburgh University Press, 1993.

BLACK, J. S., and G. W. CHRYSTAL. *The Life of William Robertson Smith.* London: A. & C. Black, 1912.

CAIRNS, DAVID S. *David Cairns: An Autobiography.* Edited by D. Cairns and A. H. Cairns. London: S.C.M. Press, 1950.

CANDLISH, R. S. *The Fatherhood of God.* 2nd ed. 1865.

CHADWICK, O. *The Secularisation of the European Mind in the Nineteenth Century.* Cambridge: Cambridge University Press, 1975.

CHALMERS, THOMAS. *A Series of Discourses on the Christian Revelation: Viewed in Connection with the Modern Astronomy.* 4th ed. Glasgow: James Hedderwick, 1817.

———. *The Evidence and Authority of the Christian Revelation.* Edinburgh, 1814.

CHALMERS, THOMAS. "Institutes of Theology." In *Posthumous Works of the Reverend Thomas Chalmers*. Edited by W. Hanna. Edinburgh: Sutherland & Knox, 1849.

COFFEY, JOHN. "Democracy and Popular Religion: Moody and Sankey's Mission to Britain, 1873–1875." In *Citizenship and Community: Liberals, Radicals and Collective Identities in the British Isles, 1865–1931*, edited by Eugenio F. Biagini, pp. 93–119. Cambridge and New York: Cambridge University Press, 1996.

CORMACK, M. J. *The Stirling Tract Enterprise and the Drummonds*. Stirling: University of Stirling Bibliographical Society, 1984.

DARLOW, T. H. *William Robertson Nicoll: Life and Letters*. London: Hodder & Stoughton, 1925.

DENNEY, J. On *"Natural Law in the Spiritual World" by a Brother of the Natural Man*. London: A. Gardner, 1885.

DESMOND, ADRIAN. *The Politics of Evolution: Morphology, Medicine and Reform in Radical London*. Chicago: University of Chicago Press, 1989.

DICK, THOMAS. *The Christian Philosopher*. Glasgow: Collins, 1846.

DRUMMOND, A. L., and J. BULLOCH. *The Church in Late Victorian Scotland 1874–1900*. Edinburgh: St. Andrew Press, 1978.

DRUMMOND, H. "A Visit to Mr. Moody and Mr. Sankey." *New Zealand Christian Record*, 1880.

———. *Natural Law in the Spiritual World*. London: Hodder & Stoughton, 1884.

———. *Stones Rolled Away and Other Addresses to Young Men Delivered in America*. New York: J. Pott & Co., 1899; London: S. Bagster, 1903.

———. *The Ascent of Man*. London: Hodder & Stoughton, 1894.

———. *The Evolution of Bible Study*, edited by A. Fleming. New York, 1901.

———. *The Greatest Thing in the World*. London: Hodder & Stoughton, 1890.

DRUMMOND, H. *The Ideal Life and Other Unpublished Addresses with Memorial Sketches by Ian Maclaren [pseud] and W. Robertson Nicoll.* 3rd ed. London: Hodder & Stoughton, 1899.

——. *The New Evangelism and Other Papers.* 2nd ed. London: Hodder & Stoughton, 1899.

——. *Tropical Africa.* London: Hodder & Stoughton, 1888.

DUNS, JOHN. *Science and Christian Thought.* London: Religious Tract Society, 1866.

FINDLAY, JAMES F., JR. *Dwight L. Moody: American Evangelist, 1837–1899.* Chicago: University of Chicago Press, 1969.

HANNA, WILLIAM, ed. *Memoirs of the Life and Writings of Thomas Chalmers, D.D., LL.D.* Edinburgh: Sutherland & Knox, 1849–1852.

LAIDLAW, JOHN. *The Bible Doctrine of Man.* Edinburgh: T&T Clark, 1879.

LENNOX, C. [J. H. Napier]. *Henry Drummond: A Biographical Sketch.* 4th ed. London: Andrew Melrose, 1902.

MOFFATT, J., ed. *Letters of Principal, James Denney to His Family and Friends.* London: Hodder & Stoughton, 1922.

MOORE, A. L. *Science and the Faith: Essays on Apologetic Subjects.* London: K. Paul, Trench, 1889.

MOORE, J. R. "Evangelicals and Evolution: Henry Drummond, Herbert Spencer and the Naturalisation of the Spiritual World." *Scottish Journal of Theology* 38 (1985): 383–417.

——. *The Post-Darwinian Controversies: A Study of the Protestant Struggle to Come to Terms with Darwin in Great Britain and America, 1870–1900.* Cambridge: Cambridge University Press, 1979.

MOODY, WILLIAM R. *The Life of Dwight L. Moody.* New York: Fleming H. Revell Co., 1900.

NEEDHAM, J. *Time: The Refreshing River.* London: Allen & Unwin, 1943.

POLLOCK, J. C. *Moody: A Biographical Portrait of the Pacesetter in Modern Mass Evangelism.* New York: Macmillan, 1963.

RAINY, ROBERT. *Evolution and Theology: Inaugural Address Delivered in the New College, Edinburgh at the Opening of the Session 1874–75*. Edinburgh: Maclaren & Macniven, 1874.

RUSSELL, C. A. *Cross-currents: Interactions between Science and Faith*. Leicester: Inter-Varsity Press, 1985.

SHANKS, T. J., ed. *A College of Colleges: Led by D. L. Moody*. Chicago, 1887.

SIMPSON, J. Y. *Henry Drummond*. Edinburgh: Oliphant, Anderson, & Ferrier, 1901.

SIMPSON, P. C. *The Life of Principal Rainy*. London: Hodder & Stoughton, 1909.

SMITH, GEORGE ADAM. *The Life of Henry Drummond*. 2nd ed. London: Hodder & Stoughton, 1899.

SMITH, LILIAN A. *George Adam Smith: A Personal Memoir and Family Chronicle*. London: Hodder & Stoughton, 1944.

SPRINGHALL, J., B. FRASER, and M. HOARE. *Sure and Stedfast: A History of the Boys' Brigade, 1883 to 1983*. London: Collins, 1983.

TOONE, MARK J. "Evangelicalism in Transition: A Comparative Analysis of the Work and Theology of D. L. Moody and His Proteges, Henry Drummond and R. A. Torrey." Ph.D. diss., St. Andrews University, 1988.

TULLOCH, J. "Theological Controversy" (An address delivered to the Theological Society in the University of Edinburgh). Edinburgh: William Blackwood & Sons, 1865.

WATSON, JOHN [Ian Maclaren]. "Henry Drummond." *North American Review* 164 (1897): 513–525.

WYSONG, J. M. "Henry Drummond." In *Dictionary of Scottish Church History and Theology*, edited by N. M. de S. Cameron. Edinburgh: T&T Clark, 1993.

A chronology of significant events in the life and history of Henry Drummond

August 17, 1851
Birth of Henry Drummond at Stirling

1863
Enters boarding school, Morison's Academy at Crieff

July, 1866
Leaves Morison's Academy at Crieff

October, 1866
Matriculates at University of Edinburgh

July 26, 1870
Passes Free Church Board Examination

November, 1870
Enters New College (Divinity) of University of Edinburgh, at age 19, youngest student in his class

November, 1872
Accepts offer of geological tutorship in University of Edinburgh by Sir (then Professor) Archibald Geikie

Summer, 1873
Enrolls for summer term at University of Tübingen, Germany

Fall, 1873
Decides to postpone divinity studies in order to gain practical experience; began service as volunteer missionary at Riego Street Mission of St. Cuthbert's Free Church, Edinburgh

April, 1874 – July, 1875
Volunteer speaker and follow-up worker in conjunction with
Moody–Sankey meetings in Scotland, England, Ireland

August, 1875
Under the influence of Mrs. George Freeland Barbour, mother
of his friend, Robert W. Barbour, decides to return to divinity
studies

Winter, 1875–1876
Forms the Gaiety Club, close circle of ministerial student
friends, so named because they originally met in the Gaiety
Music Hall, Edinburgh

April, 1876
Finishes four-year course in Divinity at New College,
University of Edinburgh, passes second part of exit
examination

December, 1876 – April, 1877
Serves as assistant during illness of the minister at Barclay
Church, Edinburgh

July, 1877
Holiday visit to Norway with Robert W. Barbour

September, 1877
To replace a deceased professor, Drummond receives a
last-minute, one-year appointment as Lecturer in Natural
Science, at Free Church College, Glasgow

Summer, 1878
Replaces chaplain at Free Church of Scotland church station
on Malta, followed by travel to Italy, Switzerland, France

Spring, 1878
Affiliates with Renfield Free Church, Glasgow under the
ministry of Dr. Marcus Dods

September, 1878
Introduced to flock of new mission station, sponsored
by Renfield Free Church in Possil Park suburb of
Glasgow

July – September, 1879
First visit to United States, a geological expedition to Rocky Mountain region with Sir Archibald Geikie; visit with Moody and Sankey in Cleveland, Ohio

April 5, 1883
Public release of *Natural Law in the Spiritual World*

June, 1883 – April, 1884
On expedition to Central Africa

October, 1883
Boys' Brigade is founded by W. A. Smith of Glasgow with Drummond as an early supporter, frequent speaker, writer, honorary vice-president

December 4, 1884
Inducted into new Chair of Natural Science (had been Lecturer), Free Church College, Glasgow

Fall, 1884 – January, 1885
Highly successful visits of C. T. Studd and Stanley Smith inspire beginning of Edinburgh student ministry

April, May, 1885
Speaks at invitational meetings for prominent persons, sponsored by the Earl and Countess of Aberdeen in Grosvenor House, London residence of the Duke and Duchess of Westminster

1885
Purchased residence at 3 Park Circus, above West End Park (now Kelvingrove Park), Glasgow

1886
Declines offer to join Lord Aberdeen's staff after Aberdeen is appointed Viceroy of Dublin; declines W. E. Gladstone's urging to stand for Parliament

Fall, 1886
Holiday to Switzerland followed by tours of German universities to tell of Edinburgh student ministry

Summer, 1887

Visit to United States; speaks at Moody's Northfield
Student Conference, Chautauqua; receives honorary
doctoral degree at Amherst College; visits Harvard, Yale,
Princeton, Wellesley, Smith, etc., to tell of student ministry;
visits with Mark Twain, Harriet Beecher Stowe; address
to the American Association for the Advancement of
Science

1887

The Greatest Thing in the World is published in *A College of
Colleges* (transcript of addresses at Moody's summer
conference at Northfield)

January 1, 1888

Death of Henry Drummond's father (also named Henry
Drummond) at Stirling

1888

Tropical Africa, an account of Drummond's African
experience, is published

June, 1888

A second set of invitational meetings for prominent persons,
sponsored by the Earl and Countess of Aberdeen in Grosvenor
House, the London residence of the Duke and Duchess of
Westminster

Summer, 1888

Holiday with family in Switzerland, later with Lord
Aberdeen; afterward travels to Venice with mother and
sisters

1889

Begins work on Glasgow University Settlement in poor
sections of Glasgow

1889

Publication of *The Greatest Thing in the World* as
separate Christmas booklet, printed to Drummond's
specifications

March – April, 1890
   Travels to Australia, to share news of Edinburgh student
   ministries; Drummond holds the hand of his former university
   classmate and now minister, John Ewing, as he suddenly
   becomes ill and dies; travels on to Fiji Islands, Manila, Java,
   Saigon, Singapore, Hong Kong, Shanghai, Tokyo

Christmas, 1890
   Publication of *Pax Vobiscum*, Christmas booklet

April – May, 1891
   Drummond travels to French Riviera to maintain
   three-week vigil at the bedside of terminally ill friend,
   Robert W. Barbour, who dies, May 17, 1891, with
   Drummond holding his hand

Christmas, 1891
   Publication of *The Programme of Christianity*, Christmas
   booklet

Winter, 1891–92
   Interim editor of children's publication, *Wee Willie Winkie*

Christmas, 1892
   Publication of *The City Without A Church*, Christmas
   booklet

March 22 – October, 1893
   Visit to United States to give Lowell Institute Lectures at
   Boston, speak at colleges, Chautauqua, visit Oliver Wendell
   Holmes, visit Moody at Northfield, visit Aberdeens in
   Quebec, fishing holiday with W. E. Dodge of New York,
   Chicago "World's Columbian Exposition," Evangelical
   Alliance of the United States which that year became known
   as the "International Christian Conference," University of
   Chicago, Addresses on behalf of Boys' Brigade

Christmas, 1893
   Publication of *The Changed Life*, Christmas booklet

May, 1894
   The Ascent of Man is published, a re-working of his Lowell
   Lectures

January, 1895
First meeting, with intent to establish "Pleasant Sunday Afternoon" series for working men of the district of Glasgow known as Port Dundas, terminus of the Edinburgh and Glasgow Canal

February, 1895
Drummond writes to Dr. Simpson that he can no longer speak at the Edinburgh student meetings because of breakdown in his health

March, 1895
Doctors forbid him to finish at end of term due to worsening illness

April – May, 1895
Drummond is taken to south of France to the baths at Dax, seeking relief; moved to Biarritz in May and then to London

September, 1895 – March, 1897
Deteriorating health despite visits of many friends and family at Tunbridge Wells

May, 1895
Drummond survives criticism over his views on the theory of evolution after his writings provoke consideration by General Assembly of the Free Church of Scotland

March 11, 1897
Death at 11 a.m. at Tunbridge Wells; funeral is held March 15, 1897 in Stirling

1897
Publication of *The Ideal Life* with biographical sketches by W. Robertson Nicoll and John Watson (Ian Maclaren)

1898
Publication of *The Monkey That Would Not Kill*, short children's story originally written for *Wee Willie Winkie* Magazine

1899
Publication of *The Life of Henry Drummond* by his friend and colleague, George Adam Smith

1899
Publication of *Stones Rolled Away, and Other Addresses to Young Men Delivered in America*

1901
Publication of *Henry Drummond* by James Y. Simpson in the "Famous Scots Series"

1901
Publication of *Henry Drummond: A Biographical Sketch* by Cuthbert Lennox (J. H. Napier)

1902
Under sponsorship of Lord and Lady Aberdeen, installation of Drummond Memorial fountain with sculpture by James Pittendrigh Macgillivray; at ceremony with commemorative poem by H. D. Rawnsley in West End Park (Kelvingrove Park), Glasgow (see page 122)

1953
Publication of *Henry Drummond: An Anthology* by James W. Kennedy, first new Drummond publication in fifty years

March, 1997
Publication of *The Greatest Thing in the World*, Henry Drummond Centennial edition

March 14, 1997
Henry Drummond Centenary Symposium, at New College, University of Edinburgh, sponsored by Beeson Divinity School of Samford University, Birmingham, Alabama, U.S.A.; the University of St. Andrews, Scotland; New College, University of Edinburgh, Scotland

October 16, 1997
Unveiling of Drummond busts by sculptor Glyn Acree

October 16–17, 1997
Henry Drummond in America: A Centennial Celebration, at Beeson Divinity School of Samford University, Birmingham, Alabama, U.S.A., sponsored by the University of St. Andrews, Scotland; New College, University of Edinburgh, Scotland; Beeson Divinity School of Samford University, Birmingham, Alabama, U.S.A.

Index

139